Underground Railroad Sampler

Eleanor Burns & Sue Bouchard

For the Brave Runaways
that risked their lives for Freedom!

First printing February, 2003
Published by Quilt in a Day®, Inc.
1955 Diamond St, San Marcos, CA 92078
©2003 by Eleanor A. Burns Family Trust
ISBN 1-891776-13-4
Art Director Merritt Voigtlander

Table of Contents

Introduction

The history of the Underground Railroad has always fascinated me. In my classes, I've often spoken of the history hidden in quilts, such as the way a Log Cabin block was used to signal a "safe house" for runaway slaves. When I found a book called *Hidden in Plain View*, by Jacqueline Tobin and Raymond Dobard, Ph.D., I learned that certain quilt blocks were possibly used as a code to guide slaves to freedom.

In 1994, Jacqueline Tobin met a woman named Ozella McDaniel Williams, from South Carolina, who told her that quilts were used to communicate information about the Underground Railroad. She remembered the code this way:

"The monkey wrench turns the wagon wheel toward Canada on a bear's paw trail to the crossroads. Once they got to the crossroads, they dug a log cabin on the ground. Shoofly told them to dress up in cotton and satin bow ties, go to the cathedral church, get married and exchange double wedding rings. Flying geese stay on the drunkard's path and follow the stars."

According to Ozella and her family's oral history, there were ten quilts used to direct the slaves to get ready for escape. Ozella also mentioned a number of secondary patterns. Each of the blocks had a different meaning and part to play in the code. The quilts would be hung one at a time on a fence or cabin door, left to "air out" while communicating a specific action or step in the journey.

As I studied the names of Ozella's code quilts, I searched for matching quilts made around the same time period. It made me wonder what messages could be hidden in the antique quilts I found. I conjured up all kinds of stories about the quiltmaker as I viewed her perfect, or often imperfect blocks!

Even if you find Ozella's story unbelieveable, you can still enjoy these fifteen traditional blocks. They are perfect for your own family's story telling.

May your quilting take you to freedom!

Eleanor Burns

Eleanor Burns

While Eleanor was working on her Underground Railroad video program, I became very intrigued with the oral history. The importance of the quilt blocks as a part of this movement to freedom is very believable to me. As a result, a sampler quilt featuring the ten primary codes and five of the secondary codes was a perfect way to document the blocks and share the story with others.

Right after the historical lesson about the significance of each block, there are instructions on how to make each one. You can choose to sew either the 12" blocks for a full size quilt or the 6" blocks for a smaller wallhanging.

Once your blocks are completed they can be set together with Plain Lattice and Cornerstones, or for the 12" blocks, you can choose to make the Flying Geese Lattice. For both styles, instructions and cutting charts are provided for twelve, fifteen and sixteen block quilts.

Remember to add the story label (page 159) on the front of your quilt as one of the blocks or on the back so the meaning of the blocks will never be lost.

I know you will enjoy making this sampler quilt as much as my students and I did. It gives you the perfect way to share the story with your friends and family.

Sue Bouchard

Sue Bouchard

Yardage for 15 Blocks

4 Backgrounds

 Background 1
12" Blocks
1 yd
6" Blocks
½ yd

Your fabric swatch

 Background 2
12" Blocks
¾ yd
6" Blocks
½ yd

Your fabric swatch

 Background 3
12" Blocks
¾ yd
6" Blocks
½ yd

Your fabric swatch

Background 4
12" Blocks
¾ yd
6" Blocks
½ yd

Your fabric swatch

13 Mediums and Darks

 Red 1
12" Blocks
¼ yd
6" Blocks
⅛ yd

Your fabric swatch

 Brown 1
12" Blocks
¼ yd
6" Blocks
⅛ yd

Your fabric swatch

 Green 1
12" Blocks
½ yd
6" Blocks
¼ yd

Your fabric swatch

 Blue 1
12" Blocks
½ yd
6" Blocks
¼ yd

Your fabric swatch

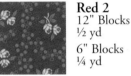 **Red 2**
12" Blocks
½ yd
6" Blocks
¼ yd

Your fabric swatch

 Brown 2
12" Blocks
¼ yd
6" Blocks
⅛ yd

Your fabric swatch

Green 2
12" Blocks
¼ yd
6" Blocks
⅛ yd

Your fabric swatch

 Blue 2
12" Blocks
½ yd
6" Blocks
¼ yd

Your fabric swatch

 Red 3
12" Blocks
¼ yd
6" Blocks
⅛ yd

Your fabric swatch

 **Brown 3**
12" Blocks
¼ yd
6" Blocks
⅛ yd

Your fabric swatch

 Green 3
12" Blocks
¼ yd
6" Blocks
⅛ yd

Your fabric swatch

 Blue 3
12" Blocks
¼ yd
6" Blocks
⅛ yd

Your fabric swatch

 Black
12" Blocks
⅛ yd
6" Blocks
⅛ yd

Your fabric swatch

Select four different Background fabrics of similar values. Tone on tone prints in different scales work the best. In addition, select thirteen medium to dark fabrics. Again, tone on tone prints in different scales plus fabrics that read solid from a distance work the best. Vary the scales for more interest. For authenticity, work with reproduction fabric lines designated as 1840 - 1880. Label your fabrics as you purchase them.

Borders and Finishing for 12" Blocks

Yardage is sufficient for 12, 15, or 16 block layouts.

12 Blocks   61" x 76"   *Sue Bouchard*

Flying Geese Lattice

Print	Flying Geese	Flying Geese & Cornerstones	Second Border Non-Stripe	or	Second Border Stripes	Binding	Batting and Backing
3¼ yds	½ yd	¾ yd	1½ yds		3 yds	1 yd	Purchase after the top is Finished

12" Blocks with Plain Lattice

Yardage is sufficient for 12, 15, or 16 block layouts.

15 Blocks 60" x 90"   Eleanor Burns

12" Blocks with Plain Lattice

Lattice	Cornerstones	Border Non-Stripe	or	Stripe	Binding	Batting and Backing
1½ yds	¼ yd	1½ yds		3 yds	1 yd	Purchase after the top is Finished

6" Blocks with Plain Lattice

Yardage is sufficient for 12, 15, or 16 block layouts.

16 Blocks 34" x 34"   Sue Bouchard

6" Blocks with Plain Lattice

Lattice	Cornerstones	Border Non-Stripe	or	Stripe	Binding	Batting and Backing
¾ yd	⅛ yd	½ yd		1¼ yds	½ yd	Purchase after the top is Finished

Supplies

Large Flying Geese Ruler

Use green lines for 4" x 8" finished geese and red lines for 2" x 4" finished geese.

Block that requires large flying geese ruler is:
    Flying Geese

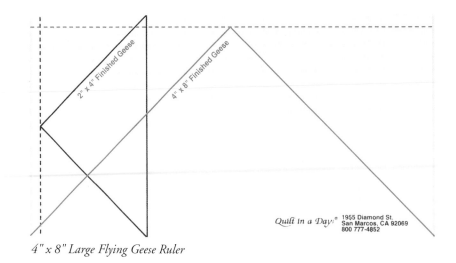

4" x 8" Large Flying Geese Ruler

Small Flying Geese Ruler

Use green lines for 3" x 6" finished geese and red lines for 1½" x 3" finished geese.

Blocks that require small flying geese ruler are:
    Carpenter's Wheel
    North Star

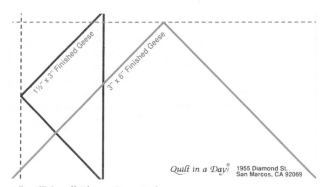

3" x 6" Small Flying Geese Ruler

6½" Triangle Square Up Ruler

Use to check size of 6½" blocks, and square up triangle pieced squares.

Blocks that require 6½" ruler are:
    Underground Railroad
    Monkey Wrench
    Carpenter's Wheel
    Bear's Paw
    Basket
    Shoo-Fly
    Bow Tie
    Birds in the Air
    Sailboat

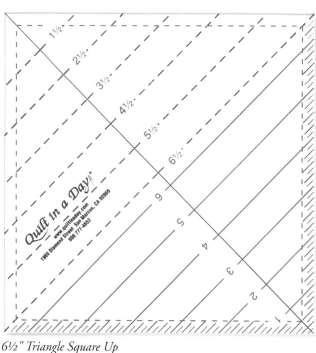

6½" Triangle Square Up

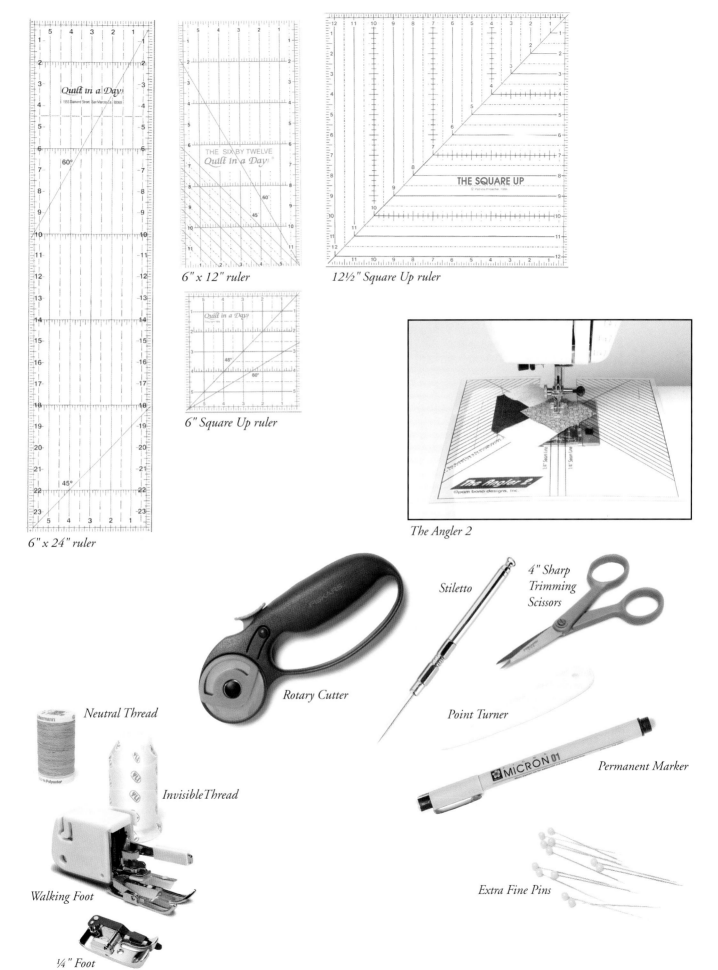

6" x 12" ruler

12½" Square Up ruler

6" Square Up ruler

The Angler 2

6" x 24" ruler

Neutral Thread

Invisible Thread

Walking Foot

¼" Foot

Rotary Cutter

Stiletto

4" Sharp Trimming Scissors

Point Turner

Permanent Marker

Extra Fine Pins

Cutting Your Quilt

The second page of each block shows a color photograph of the block, the suggested fabric to use for each piece, and the size to cut from that suggested fabric for both the 12" and 6" finished blocks.

You can individually cut each block, or you can assembly-line cut all pieces for all fifteen blocks before you begin sewing. Assembly-line cutting is the best use of time and fabric, but does take several hours time. Once cutting is completed, each block takes approximately one hour or less.

Fabrics based on the yardage charts have been equally distributed throughout the blocks. If you choose to use fabrics other than the 1840 – 1880 reproduction fabrics, assign your fabric to a fabric in the chart.

Cutting Strips for Individual Blocks

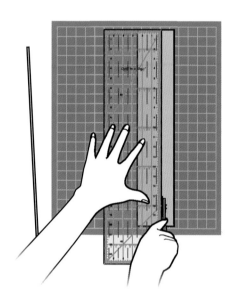

1. Select designated fabric according to individual chart, and press.

2. Select ruler slightly longer than designated size. Best rulers to use for strips are the 6" x 24" ruler and 6" x 12" ruler. Straighten left edge, selvage to selvage.

3. Move ruler over until ruler lines are at newly cut edge. Carefully and accurately line up and cut strips at measurements given.

Cutting Squares and Rectangles

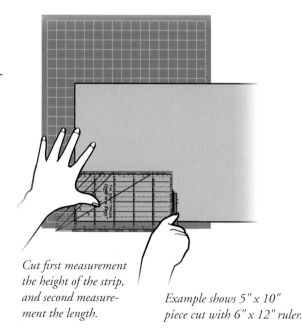

1. Select ruler slightly larger than designated size. Best rulers to use for cutting squares and rectangles are the 6" x 12", and 6" and 12½" Square Up rulers. Place ruler on left corner of fabric, lining up ruler with grain of fabric.

2. Rotary cut pieces on right side of ruler, and across top, slightly larger than designated size.

3. Turn piece and cut to exact size.

Cut first measurement the height of the strip, and second measurement the length.

Example shows 5" x 10" piece cut with 6" x 12" ruler.

Assembly-line Cutting Fifteen Blocks

1. Make photocopies of all labels on pages 160-167 onto Avery Labels #5760, available at most office supply stores.

2. Label a plastic quart size bag with name of each block.

3. Begin with Background #1, page 14. Straighten left edge.

4. Cut first strip indicated width, selvage to selvage, with 6" x 24" ruler. Use grid on cutting mat for measurement.

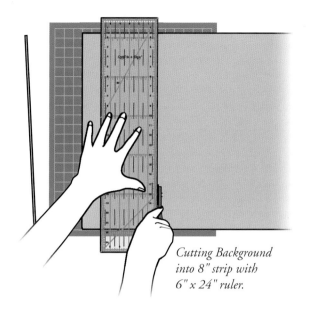

Cutting Background into 8" strip with 6" x 24" ruler.

5. Turn strip and straighten left edge. Cut strip into indicated sizes of squares and rectangles.

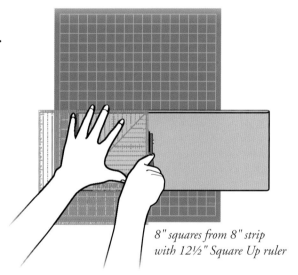

8" squares from 8" strip with 12½" Square Up ruler

7. Place a label on each piece and put into appropriate block's bag.

8. Continue cutting and labeling each piece of fabric, and placing in appropriate bag.

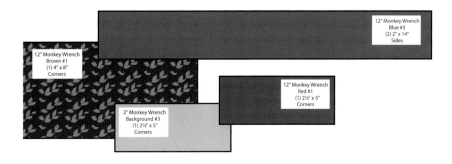

12" Block

Background #1   1 yd

(1) 8" strip cut into
(1) 8" square	Basket
(1) 7" square	Basket
(1) 7" square	Flying Geese
(2) 7¼" squares	Drunkard's Path

(1) 5½" strip cut into
(2) 5½" squares	Drunkard's Path
(3) 5½" squares	Crossroads
(1) 5" x 10"	Railroad

(1) 3½" strip cut into
(2) 3½" x 6½"	Basket
(2) 3½" squares	Crossroads

(2) 2½" strips cut into
(9) 2½" squares	Crossroads
(1) 2½" x 30"	Railroad

(1) 1¾" strip cut into
(1) 1¾" x 5"	Log Cabin
(1) 1¾" x 6¼"	Log Cabin

Paste your Background #1 fabric here

6" Block

Background #1   ½ yd

(1) 5" strip cut into
(1) 5" square	Basket
(1) 4" square	Basket
(2) 4¼" squares	Drunkard's Path
(2) 3" squares	Drunkard's Path
(1) 3" x 6"	Railroad

(1) 3½" strip cut into
(3) 3½" squares	Crossroads
(2) 2" x 3½"	Basket
(1) 1⅛" x 2¾"	Log Cabin
(1) 1⅛" x 3⅜"	Log Cabin
(2) 2" squares	Crossroads

(2) 1½" strips into
(9) 1½" squares	Crossroads
(1) 1½" x 20"	Railroad
(8) 1½" squares	Flying Geese

Paste your Background #1 fabric here

Background #2   ¾ yd

(1) 13" strip cut into
(1) 13" square	Wagon Wheel
(1) 7½" square	North Star
(1) 6" square	Birds
(5) 5½" squares	Bow Tie

(1) 3½" strip cut into
(4) 3½" squares	North Star
(3) 2½" x 3¼"	Birds
(1) 1¾" x 2½"	Log Cabin
(1) 1¾" x 3¾"	Log Cabin

Paste your Background #2 fabric here

Background #2   ¾ yd

(1) 7" strip cut into
(1) 7" square	Wagon Wheel
(1) 4½" square	North Star
(1) 4" square	Birds
(5) 3½" squares	Bow Tie

(1) 2" strip cut into
(4) 2" squares	North Star
(3) 1½" x 2¼"	Birds
(1) 1⅛" x 1½"	Log Cabin
(1) 1⅛" x 2⅛"	Log Cabin

Paste your Background #2 fabric here

12" Block

Background #3	¾ yd
(1) 7" strip cut into	
(1) 7" square	Flying Geese
(1) 6" square	Birds
(2) 6" squares	Shoo-Fly
(1) 4½" strip cut into	
(2) 4½" squares	Carpenter's Wheel
(1) 4½" square	North Star
(2) 4" squares	Sailboat
(1) 3½" strip cut into	
(3) 3½" squares	Sailboat
(2) 3½" x 6½"	Sailboat
(4) 3½" squares	Carpenter's Wheel
(1) 2½" strip cut into	
(10) 2½" squares	Shoo-Fly
(3) 2½" x 3¼"	Birds
(1) 2½" x 5"	Monkey Wrench
(1) 2" strip cut into	
(4) 2" squares	North Star
(8) 2" squares	Carpenter's Wheel
(4) 2" x 3½"	Carpenter's Wheel
(1) 1¾" strip cut into	
(1) 1¾" x 7½"	Log Cabin
(1) 1¾" x 8¾"	Log Cabin
(1) 1¼" x 15"	Monkey Wrench

Paste your Background #3 fabric here

6" Block

Background #3	½ yd
(1) 4" strip cut into	
(1) 4" square	Birds
(2) 4" squares	Shoo-Fly
(2) 2½" squares	Sailboat
(2) 2½" x 3½"	Sailboat
(3) 2" squares	Sailboat
(4) 2" squares	Carpenter's Wheel
(1) 2" x 4"	Monkey Wrench
(1) 1½" strip cut into	
(8) 1½" squares	Flying Geese
(10) 1½" squares	Shoo-Fly
(3) 1½" x 2¼"	Birds
(1) 1¼" strip cut into	
(4) 1¼" x 2"	North Star
(4) 1¼" squares	North Star
(8) 1¼" squares	Carpenter's Wheel
(8) 1¼" x 2"	Carpenter's Wheel
(4) 1¼" x 2"	Carpenter's Wheel
(1) 1⅛" x 4"	Log Cabin
(1) 1⅛" x 4⅝"	Log Cabin
(1) ⅞" x 9"	Monkey Wrench

Paste your Background #3 fabric here

Background #4	¾ yd
(1) 7" strip cut into	
(1) 7" square	Flying Geese
(2) 6" squares	Bear's Paw
(1) 4" strip cut into	
(1) 4" x 8"	Monkey Wrench
(1) 3½" square	Monkey Wrench
(4) 2¼" squares	Bear's Paw
(2) 2" strips cut into	
(4) 2" x 5¾"	Bear's Paw
(1) 2" x 10"	Log Cabin
(1) 2" x 11¼"	Log Cabin
(2) 2" x 14"	Monkey Wrench

Paste your Background #4 fabric here

Background #4	½ yd
(1) 4" strip cut into	
(2) 4" squares	Bear's Paw
(1) 2½" x 5"	Monkey Wrench
(1) 2" square	Monkey Wrench
(8) 1½" squares	Flying Geese
(1) 1⅜" strip cut into	
(4) 1⅜" squares	Bear's Paw
(1) 1⅜" x 5¼"	Log Cabin
(1) 1⅜" x 6⅛"	Log Cabin
(4) 1¼" x 3⅛"	Bear's Paw
(1) 1¼" x 15"	Monkey Wrench

Paste your Background #4 fabric here

12" Block

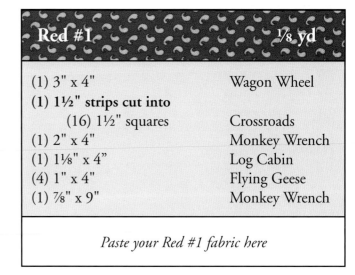

Red #1   ¼ yd

(1) 2½" strip cut into
(16) 2½" squares   Crossroads
(1) 5" x 6"   Wagon Wheel
(1) 2½" x 5"   Monkey Wrench
(1) 1¾" x 7½"   Log Cabin
(4) 1½" x 7"   Flying Geese
(1) 1¼" x 15"   Monkey Wrench

Paste your Red #1 fabric here

6" Block

Red #1   ⅛ yd

(1) 3" x 4"   Wagon Wheel
(1) 1½" strips cut into
(16) 1½" squares   Crossroads
(1) 2" x 4"   Monkey Wrench
(1) 1⅛" x 4"   Log Cabin
(4) 1" x 4"   Flying Geese
(1) ⅞" x 9"   Monkey Wrench

Paste your Red #1 fabric here

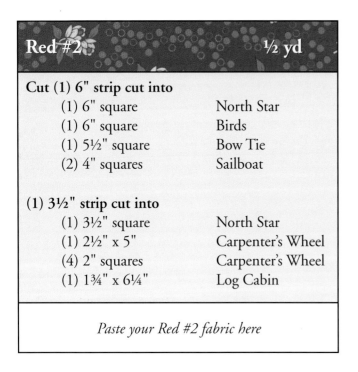

Red #2   ½ yd

Cut (1) 6" strip cut into
(1) 6" square   North Star
(1) 6" square   Birds
(1) 5½" square   Bow Tie
(2) 4" squares   Sailboat

(1) 3½" strip cut into
(1) 3½" square   North Star
(1) 2½" x 5"   Carpenter's Wheel
(4) 2" squares   Carpenter's Wheel
(1) 1¾" x 6¼"   Log Cabin

Paste your Red #2 fabric here

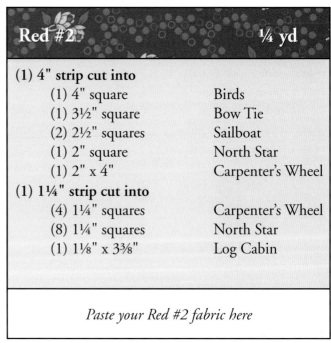

Red #2   ¼ yd

(1) 4" strip cut into
(1) 4" square   Birds
(1) 3½" square   Bow Tie
(2) 2½" squares   Sailboat
(1) 2" square   North Star
(1) 2" x 4"   Carpenter's Wheel
(1) 1¼" strip cut into
(4) 1¼" squares   Carpenter's Wheel
(8) 1¼" squares   North Star
(1) 1⅛" x 3⅜"   Log Cabin

Paste your Red #2 fabric here

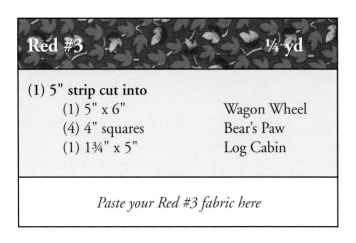

Red #3   ¼ yd

(1) 5" strip cut into
(1) 5" x 6"   Wagon Wheel
(4) 4" squares   Bear's Paw
(1) 1¾" x 5"   Log Cabin

Paste your Red #3 fabric here

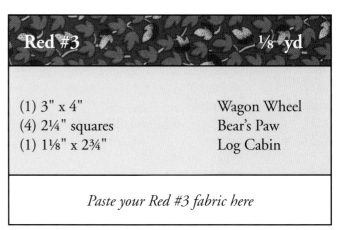

Red #3   ⅛ yd

(1) 3" x 4"   Wagon Wheel
(4) 2¼" squares   Bear's Paw
(1) 1⅛" x 2¾"   Log Cabin

Paste your Red #3 fabric here

12" Block

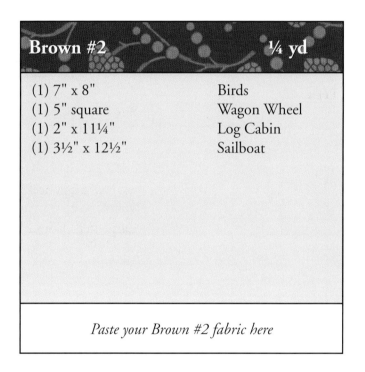

Brown #1   ¼ yd

(1) 5" x 6"	Wagon Wheel
(1) 4" x 8"	Monkey Wrench
(1) 2" x 13"	Log Cabin

Paste your Brown #1 fabric here

Brown #2   ¼ yd

(1) 7" x 8"	Birds
(1) 5" square	Wagon Wheel
(1) 2" x 11¼"	Log Cabin
(1) 3½" x 12½"	Sailboat

Paste your Brown #2 fabric here

Brown #3   ¼ yd

(1) 2½" strip cut into	
(1) 2½" x 30"	Railroad
(1) 5½" square	Bow Tie
(1) 5½" square	Flying Geese

Paste your Brown #3 fabric here

6" Block

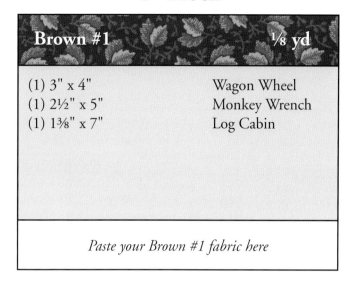

Brown #1   ⅛ yd

(1) 3" x 4"	Wagon Wheel
(1) 2½" x 5"	Monkey Wrench
(1) 1⅜" x 7"	Log Cabin

Paste your Brown #1 fabric here

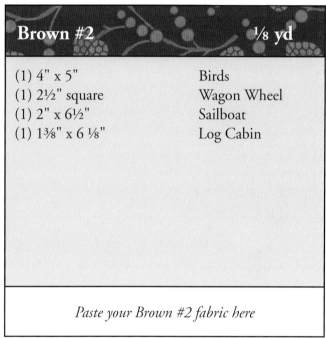

Brown #2   ⅛ yd

(1) 4" x 5"	Birds
(1) 2½" square	Wagon Wheel
(1) 2" x 6½"	Sailboat
(1) 1⅜" x 6 ⅛"	Log Cabin

Paste your Brown #2 fabric here

Brown #3   ⅛ yd

(1) 3½" square	Bow Tie
(1) 1½" x 20"	Railroad
(4) 1½" x 2½"	Flying Geese

Paste your Brown #3 fabric here

12" Block

Green #1 — ½ yd

(1) 7¼" strip cut into
- (2) 7¼" squares — Drunkard's Path
- (2) 6" squares — Shoo-Fly

(1) 5½" strip cut into
- (1) 5½" square — Bow Tie
- (2) 5½" squares — Drunkard's Path
- (1) 5" x 10" — Railroad
- (1) 5" x 6" — Wagon Wheel

(1) 2½" strip cut into
- (10) 2½" squares — Shoo-Fly
- (1) 1¾" x 8¾" — Log Cabin

Paste your Green #1 fabric here

Green #2 — ¼ yd

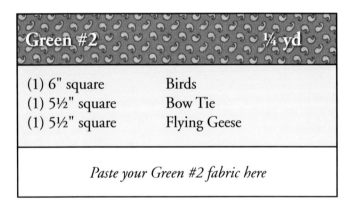

- (1) 6" square — Birds
- (1) 5½" square — Bow Tie
- (1) 5½" square — Flying Geese

Paste your Green #2 fabric here

Green #3 — ¼ yd

- (2) 6" squares — Bear's Paw

Paste your Green #3 fabric here

Black — ⅛ yd

- (1) 2½" square — Log Cabin

6" Block

Green #1 — ¼ yd

(1) 4¼" strip cut into
- (2) 4¼" squares — Drunkard's Path
- (2) 4" squares — Shoo-Fly
- (1) 3" x 4" — Wagon Wheel

(1) 3½" strip cut into
- (1) 3½" square — Bow Tie
- (2) 3" squares — Drunkard's Path
- (1) 3" x 6" — Railroad
- (1) 1⅛" x 4⅝" — Log Cabin
- (10) 1½" squares — Shoo-Fly

Paste your Green #1 fabric here

Green #2 — ⅛ yd

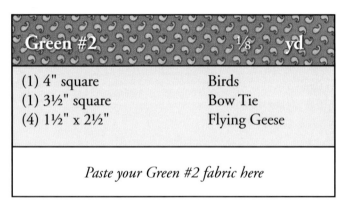

- (1) 4" square — Birds
- (1) 3½" square — Bow Tie
- (4) 1½" x 2½" — Flying Geese

Paste your Green #2 fabric here

Green #3 — ⅛ yd

- (2) 4" squares — Bear's Paw

Paste your Green #3 fabric here

Black — ⅛ yd

- (1) 1½" square — Log Cabin

12" Block

Blue #1 — ½ yd

(1) 9" strip cut into
(1) 9" square	North Star
(1) 7" x 8"	Birds
(2) 6" squares	Carpenter's Wheel

(1) 2" strip cut into
(8) 2" squares	Carpenter's Wheel
(4) 2" x 3½"	Carpenter's Wheel
(4) 2" squares	Carpenter's Wheel
(1) 2" square	Bear's Paw

(1) 3½" strip cut into
(1) 3½" square	Basket
(1) 3½" x 12½"	Sailboat
(1) 1¾" x 3¾"	Log Cabin
(4) 1½" x 7"	Flying Geese

Paste your Blue #1 fabric here

Blue #2 — ½ yd

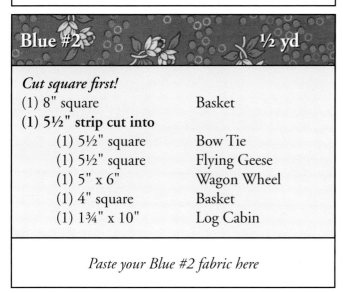

Cut square first!
(1) 8" square	Basket

(1) 5½" strip cut into
(1) 5½" square	Bow Tie
(1) 5½" square	Flying Geese
(1) 5" x 6"	Wagon Wheel
(1) 4" square	Basket
(1) 1¾" x 10"	Log Cabin

Paste your Blue #2 fabric here

Blue #3 — ¼ yd

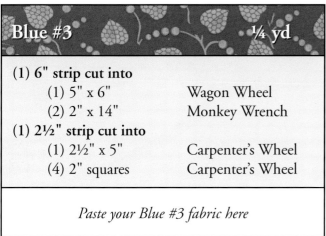

(1) 6" strip cut into
(1) 5" x 6"	Wagon Wheel
(2) 2" x 14"	Monkey Wrench

(1) 2½" strip cut into
(1) 2½" x 5"	Carpenter's Wheel
(4) 2" squares	Carpenter's Wheel

Paste your Blue #3 fabric here

6" Block

Blue #1 — ¼ yd

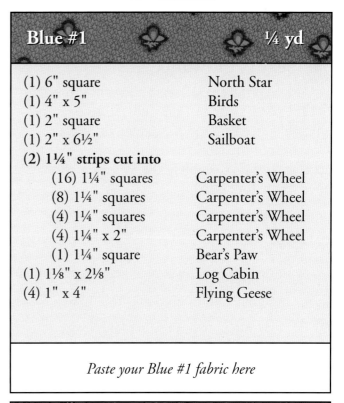

(1) 6" square	North Star
(1) 4" x 5"	Birds
(1) 2" square	Basket
(1) 2" x 6½"	Sailboat

(2) 1¼" strips cut into
(16) 1¼" squares	Carpenter's Wheel
(8) 1¼" squares	Carpenter's Wheel
(4) 1¼" squares	Carpenter's Wheel
(4) 1¼" x 2"	Carpenter's Wheel
(1) 1¼" square	Bear's Paw
(1) 1⅛" x 2⅛"	Log Cabin
(4) 1" x 4"	Flying Geese

Paste your Blue #1 fabric here

Blue #2 — ¼ yd

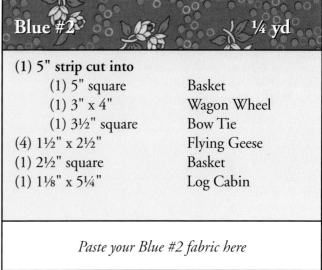

(1) 5" strip cut into
(1) 5" square	Basket
(1) 3" x 4"	Wagon Wheel
(1) 3½" square	Bow Tie
(4) 1½" x 2½"	Flying Geese
(1) 2½" square	Basket
(1) 1⅛" x 5¼"	Log Cabin

Paste your Blue #2 fabric here

Blue #3 — ⅛ yd

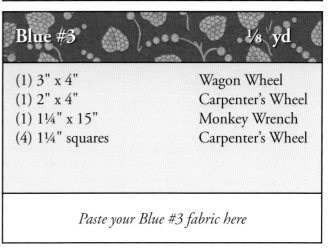

(1) 3" x 4"	Wagon Wheel
(1) 2" x 4"	Carpenter's Wheel
(1) 1¼" x 15"	Monkey Wrench
(4) 1¼" squares	Carpenter's Wheel

Paste your Blue #3 fabric here

Techniques

¼" Seam Allowance Test

Use a consistent ¼" seam allowance throughout the construction of the quilt. If necessary, adjust the needle position, change the presser foot, or feed the fabric under the presser foot to achieve the ¼". **Complete the ¼" seam allowance test before starting.**

1. Cut (3) 1½" x 6" pieces.

2. Set machine at 15 stitches per inch, or 2.0 on computerized machines.

3. Sew three strips together lengthwise with what you **think** is a ¼" seam.

4. Press seams in one direction. Make sure no folds occur at seam.

5. Place sewn sample under a ruler and measure its width. **It should measure exactly 3½".** If sample measures smaller than 3½", seam is too large. If sample measures larger than 3½", seam is too small. Adjust seam and repeat if necessary.

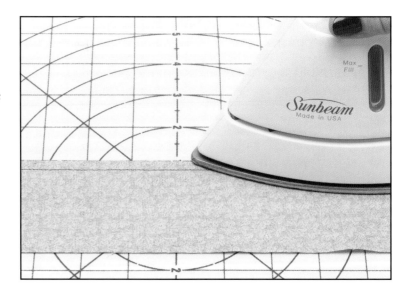

Pressing

Individual instructions usually say dark fabric should be on top, unless otherwise indicated.

1. Place on pressing mat, with fabric on top that seam is to be pressed toward. Set seam by pressing stitches.

2. Open and press against seam.

Unsewing Center Seams

Use this technique for these blocks:
    Flying Geese - page 105
    Drunkard's Path - page 120

1. At the center seam, cut the first stitch with scissors.

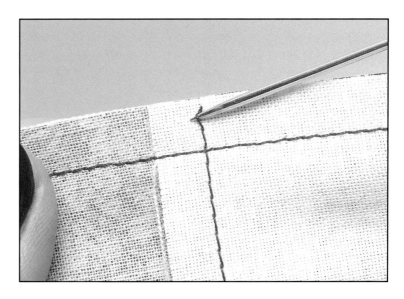

2. Remove the two or three vertical stitches at the center with stiletto or seam ripper.

3. Turn block over, and repeat removing vertical stitches at center.

4. Open the center seams and push down flat to form a tiny pinwheel.

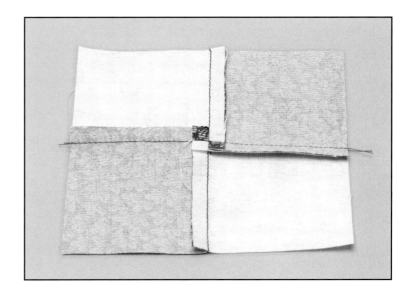

Squaring Up Triangle Pieced Squares

Triangles are oversized and need to be trimmed. This technique is called "squaring up". Use the Quilt in a Day 6½" Triangle Square Up Ruler to trim.

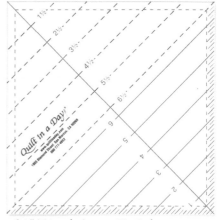

6½" Triangle Square Up Ruler

1. Stack closed triangles Background side up. If stitches show better on Triangle side, stack closed triangles Triangle side up.

2. Look for uneven edges. Freshly cut edges don't need to be trimmed. The side with the three stitches was just freshly trimmed, and should be straight. Trim the opposite side.

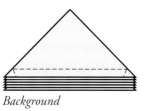

Background

3. Lay one test triangle on the cutting mat.

4. Each block indicates what size to square the patch to. Lay the ruler's indicated square up line on the seam.

5. Line up top edge of ruler with triangle. Hold ruler firmly.

6. Trim right side of triangle, pushing rotary cutter toward the point to avoid damaging the ruler's corner.

*The example shows squaring the triangle to 2½".
The ½" line on the ruler is on the stitching.*

7. Turn patch. Trim tips with rotary cutter and ruler. From stitching, trim a 45° angle.

8. Tips can also be trimmed with scissors, using a 60° angle to assure that seam allowance does not show after triangle is pressed open.

   You can also trim tips after pieced square is pressed open.

9. Lay trimmed triangle on pressing mat, triangle side up. Lift corner and press toward seam with tip of iron, pushing seams to triangle side. Press carefully so pieces do not distort.

10. Measure with 6" Square Up ruler to see if it is desired size. If not correct size, adjust placement of 6½" Triangle Square Up line before stitching if square is too small, or after stitching if square is too large.

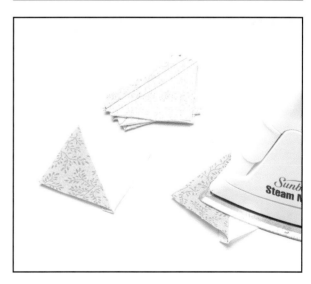

Making Dark Star Points

Use this technique in North Star, Carpenter's Wheel, and Flying Geese Lattice.

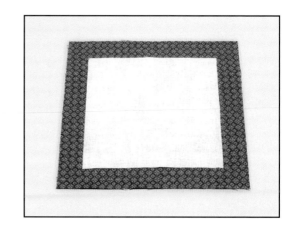

1. Place smaller square right sides together and centered on larger square.

2" x 3½" Patch	3½" x 6½" Patch
4½" Dark	7½" Dark
6" Background	9" Background

2. Place 6" x 24" ruler on squares so ruler touches all four corners. Draw diagonal line across squares. Pin.

3. Sew exactly ¼" from drawn line. Use 15 stitches per inch or 2.0 on computerized machine. Assembly-line sew several squares. Press to set seam.

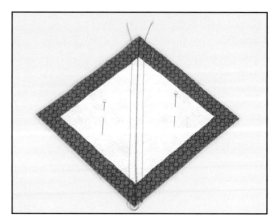

4. Remove pins. Cut on drawn line.

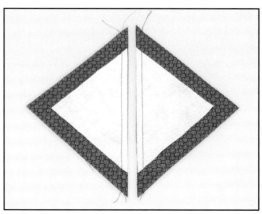

5. Place on pressing mat with large triangle on top. Press to set seam.

6. Open and press flat. Check that there are no tucks, and seam is pressed toward larger triangle.

7. Place pieces right sides together so that opposite fabrics touch with dark matched to Background. Seams are parallel with each other.

8. Match up outside edges. Notice that there is a gap between seams. The seams do not lock.

9. Draw a diagonal line across seams. Pin. Sew ¼" from both sides of drawn line. Hold seams flat with stiletto so seams do not flip. Press to set seam.

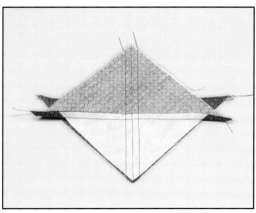

10. Cut on the drawn line.

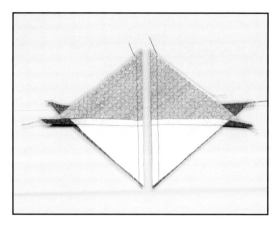

11. Fold in half and clip to the stitching. This allows the seam allowance to be pressed away from the Background triangle.

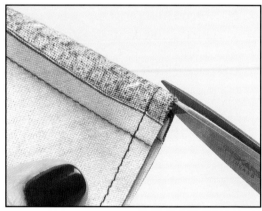

12. From right side, press into one Background triangle. Turn and press into second Background triangle.

13. Turn over, and press on wrong side. At clipped seam, fabric is pressed in opposite directions.

Squaring Up with Small Geese Ruler
2" x 3½" Patches Finished at 1½" x 3"

1. Line up ruler's red lines on 45° sewn lines. Line up dotted line with peak of triangle for ¼" seam allowance. Cut block in half to separate two patches.

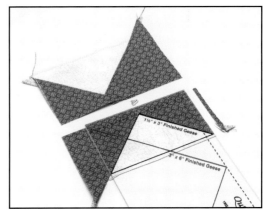

2. Trim off excess fabric on right. Hold ruler securely on fabric so it will not shift while cutting.

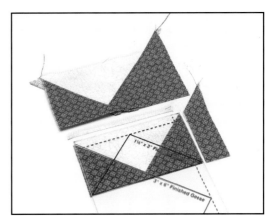

3. Turn patch around. Do not turn ruler. Trim off excess fabric on right and top.

4. Repeat with second half.

Squaring Up with Small Geese Ruler
3½" x 6½" Patches Finished at 3" x 6"

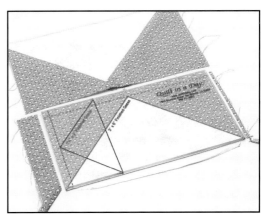

1. Line up ruler's green lines on 45° sewn lines.
2. Trim excess fabric on all four sides.

Making Flying Geese

1. Place smaller square right sides together and centered on larger square. Place 6" x 24" ruler on squares so ruler touches all four corners. Draw diagonal line across squares. Pin.

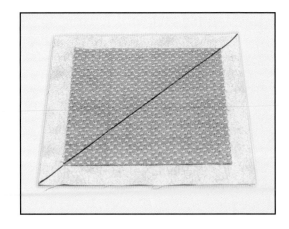

2. Sew exactly ¼" from drawn line. Use 15 stitches per inch or 2.0 on computerized machine. Assembly-line sew several squares. Press to set seam.

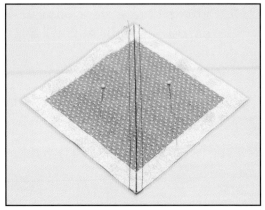

3. Remove pins. Cut on drawn line.

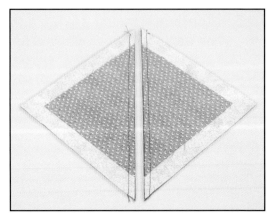

4. Place on pressing mat with large triangle on top. Press to set seam.

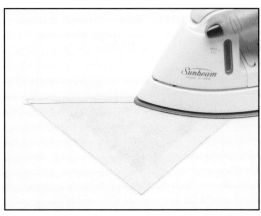

5. Open and press flat. Check that there are no tucks, and seam is pressed toward larger triangle.

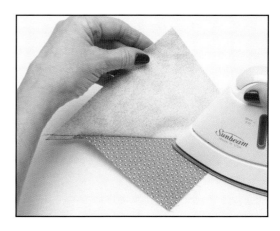

6. Place pieces right sides together so that opposite fabrics touch with dark matched to light. Seams are parallel with each other.

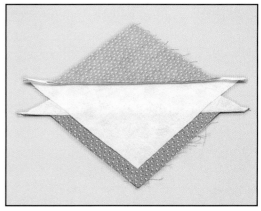

7. Match up outside edges. Notice that there is a gap between seams. The seams do not lock.

8. Draw a diagonal line across seams. Pin. Sew ¼" from both sides of drawn line. Hold seams flat with stiletto so seams do not flip. Press to set seam.

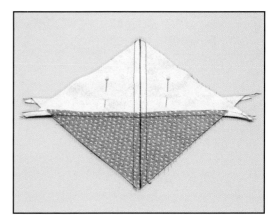

9. Cut on the drawn line.

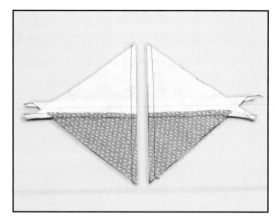

10. Fold in half and clip to the stitching. This allows the seam allowance to be pressed away from the dark triangle.

11. From right side, press into one dark triangle. Turn and press into second dark triangle.

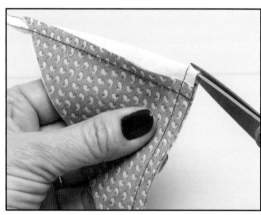

12. Turn over, and press on wrong side. At clipped seam, fabric is pressed in opposite directions.

Squaring Up with Large Geese Ruler
2½" x 4½" Patches Finished at 2" x 4"

Small Patches

1. Line up ruler's red lines on 45° sewn lines. Line up dotted line with peak of triangle for ¼" seam allowance. Cut block in half to separate two patches.

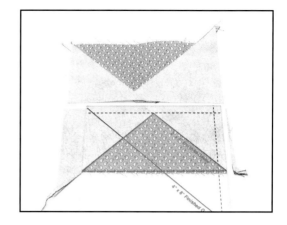

2. Trim off excess fabric on right. Hold ruler securely on fabric so it will not shift while cutting.

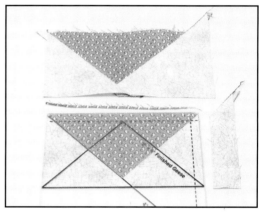

3. Turn patch around. Do not turn ruler. Trim off excess fabric on right and top.

4. Repeat with second half.

Underground Railroad

Also known as Jacob's Ladder, this block has an alternating path of dark and light that can be used to show a direction.

There is a story about a slave owner chasing a runaway who swore the man vanished as if he had stepped on some kind of "underground railroad." The idea of an Underground Railroad taking people north to freedom was used to describe the network of abolitionists and safe houses that helped slaves escape to Ohio and Canada. Safe houses along the way were known as "stations," those who guided the escapees were called "conductors" and the runaways themselves were called "passengers."

Harriet Tubman was one of the best-known conductors on the Underground Railroad. After she made her escape from slavery, Tubman returned to the South a total of 19 times to bring over 300 fugitives to freedom. She never lost a single passenger. It was her mission to guide them through unknown lands and take care of their needs. She would tell them to wait in the woods while she went to the home of a friend to buy needed provisions. She would not return until nightfall, using a song to communicate safety or danger to those hiding in wait.

Reaching a "station" in the North meant food, clothing, and a place to hide when capture was imminent. But it did not yet mean freedom. The Underground Railroad took them all the way to Canada in some cases. Estimates are that as many as 100,000 people escaped slavery between the American Revolution and the Civil War.

Skill Level
Easy

Tools to Gather
6" x 12" ruler
6½" Triangle Square Up ruler
permanent marking pen
stiletto

		12" Finished Size	6" Finished Size
Background #1			
	Four-Patches	(1) 2½" x 30"	(1) 1½" x 20"
	Triangle Pieced Squares	(1) 5" x 10"	(1) 3" x 6"
Brown #3			
	Four-Patches	(1) 2½" x 30"	(1) 1½" x 20"
Green #1			
	Triangle Pieced Squares	(1) 5" x 10"	(1) 3" x 6"

Making Five Four-Patches

1. Sew Background strip right sides together to dark strip. Set seam, open, and press seam toward dark.

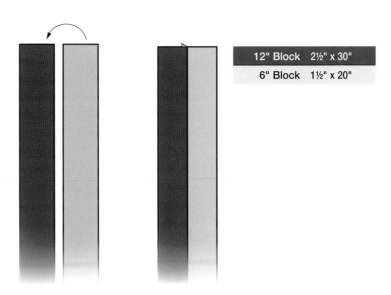

12" Block	2½" x 30"
6" Block	1½" x 20"

2. Cut sewn strips in half.

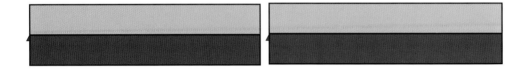

3. Layer strip sets right sides together so seams lock. Background fabrics should be touching dark fabrics.

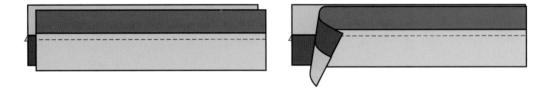

4. Layer cut five segments. **Do not separate patches after they are cut.**

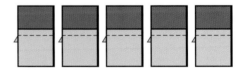

5. Assembly-line sew. Set seams and press open.

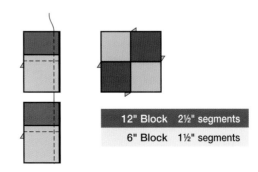

12" Block	2½" segments
6" Block	1½" segments

Making Four Triangle Pieced Squares

1. Place Background rectangle right sides together with Triangle rectangle. Press.

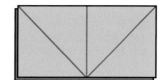

12" Block	5" x 10"
6" Block	3" x 6"

2. Place on gridded cutting mat. Draw center line and one diagonal line in each square. Pin.

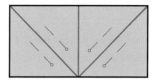

3. Sew ¼" from both sides of drawn line. Set seams.

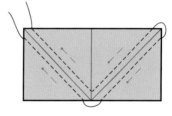

4. Cut apart on all drawn lines.

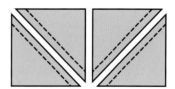

5. Square patches with Triangle Square Up ruler. Press seams toward darker of the two fabrics. See pages 22-23.

12" Block	4½" square
6" Block	2½" square

Completing the Block

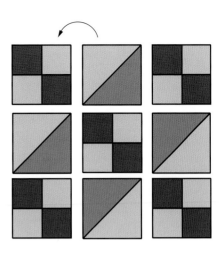

1. Lay out pieces to complete block.

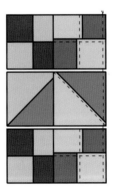

2. Flip middle vertical row right sides together to left vertical row.

3. Assembly-line sew. Do not clip connecting threads.

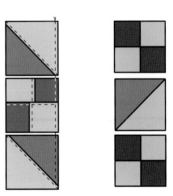

4. Flip right vertical row to middle vertical row.

5. Assembly-line sew. Do not clip connecting threads.

6. Press seams toward Four-Patches.

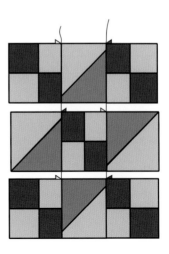

7. Turn and sew remaining rows together.

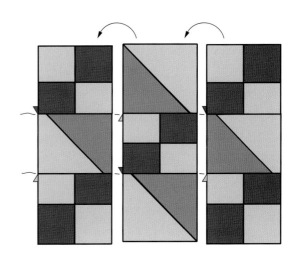

8. Lock seams and press toward Four-Patches.

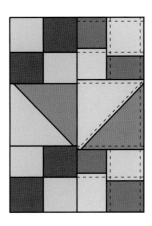

9. Press last seams away from middle row.

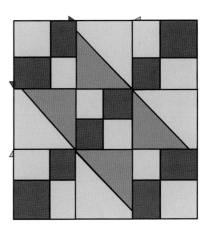

Monkey Wrench

The Monkey Wrench Quilt was the first quilt displayed as a signal for any slaves who planned to escape. The monkey wrench is a heavy metal tool used by the blacksmith. This quilt symbolized the time to collect tools they would need on their journey north to freedom.

There were physical tools needed: tools for constructing a physical shelter, tools for defending themselves, and tools for determining direction. Along with food and a few coins, they were to wrap these tools in a bandanna bundle.

They needed mental tools as well, as being cunning and alert, plus knowledge and ability to discern motives of strangers.

The blacksmith, the most knowledgeable person on the plantation, was known as the "Monkey Wrench." He had strong, skillful hands, and could talk to the slaves by the rhythmic hitting of the hammer on the anvil. The "monkey wrench" might be loaned out to neighboring plantations, so he knew the lay of the land. This person was also familiar with the daily operations of the plantation, and would not arouse suspicion.

Frederick Douglass, a well known abolitionist, was a free black "monkey wrench". Found in his home in Cedar Hill, Washington, D. C., was a Monkey Wrench family quilt.

Monkey wrench was a person or group of people who turned the wagon wheel.

Skill Level
Easy

Tools to Gather
6" x 12" ruler
6½" Triangle Square Up ruler
permanent marking pen
stiletto

		12" Finished Size	6" Finished Size
Inner Wrench			
Background #3			
	Corners	(1) 2½" x 5"	(1) 2" x 4"
	Sides	(1) 1¼" x 15"	(1) ⅞" x 9"
Red #1			
	Corners	(1) 2½" x 5"	(1) 2" x 4"
	Sides	(1) 1¼" x 15"	(1) ⅞" x 9"
Background #4			
	Center Square	(1) 3½" square	(1) 2" square
Outer Wrench			
Background #4			
	Corners	(1) 4" x 8"	(1) 2½" x 5"
	Sides	(2) 2" x 14"	(2) 1¼" x 15"
Brown #1			
	Corners	(1) 4" x 8"	(1) 2½" x 5"
Blue #3			
	Sides	(2) 2" x 14"	(1) 1¼" x 15"

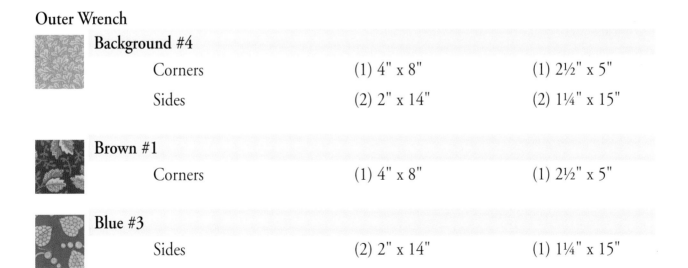

Making the Inner Wrench

Making Four Small Wrench Corners

1. Place Background rectangle right sides together to Inner Wrench rectangle. Press.

12" Block	2½" x 5"
6" Block	2" x 4"

2. Place on gridded cutting mat. Draw center line and one diagonal line in each square. Pin.

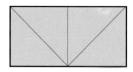

12" Block	2½" grid
6" Block	2" grid

3. Sew ¼" from both sides of diagonal lines. Set seams.

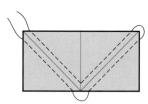

4. Cut apart on all diagonal lines.

5. Square patches with Triangle Square Up ruler. Press seams toward dark fabric. See page 22 - 23.

12" Block	2" squares
6" Block	1¼" squares

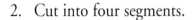 Making Four Side Strips

1. Sew Inner Wrench strip right sides together to Background strip. Set seams with darkest on top, open, and press toward darkest.

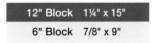

12" Block	1¼" x 15"
6" Block	7/8" x 9"

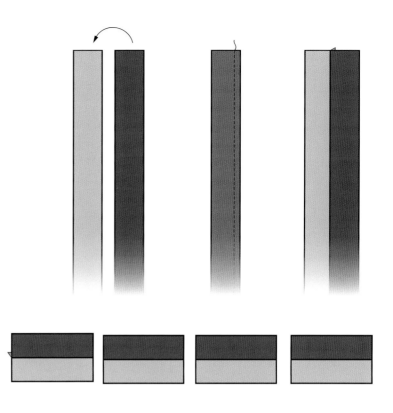

2. Cut into four segments.

12" Block	3½" segments
6" Block	2" segments

Sewing Inner Wrench Together

1. Lay out all pieces for Inner Wrench.

12" Block	3½" center
6" Block	2" center

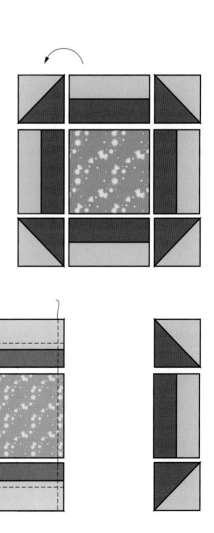

2. Flip middle row over row on left. Assembly-line sew.

3. Open and sew row on right.

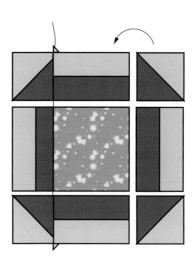

4. Turn and sew remaining rows together, locking and pressing seams toward Side strips.

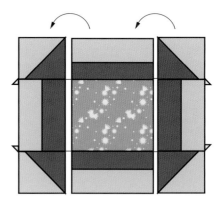

5. Set seams and press toward Center Row.

6. Measure Inner Monkey Wrench.

12" Block	6½" square
6" Block	3½" square

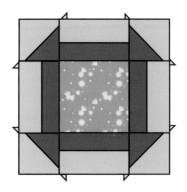

Making the Outer Wrench

Making Four Large Wrench Corners

1. Place Background rectangle right sides together to Wrench Corners rectangle. Press.

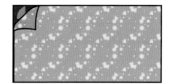

12" Block	4" x 8"
6" Block	2½" x 5"

2. Place on a gridded cutting mat. Draw center line and one diagonal line in each square. Pin.

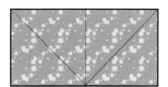

12" Block	4" grid
6" Block	2½" grid

3. Sew ¼" from both sides of diagonal lines. Set seams.

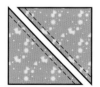

4. Cut apart on all drawn lines.

5. Square up patches with Triangle Square Up ruler. Press seams toward dark fabric.

 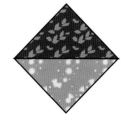

12" Block	3½" square
6" Block	2" square

Making Four Side Strips

12" Block	2" x 14"
6" Block	1¼" x 15"

1. Sew Outer Wrench strip right sides together to Background strip. Set and press seams toward dark fabric.

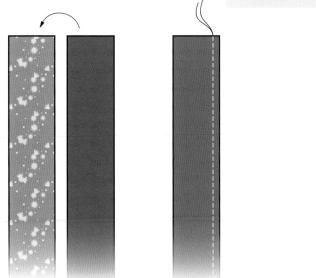

2. Cut into four segments.

12" Block	6½" segments
6" Block	3½" segments

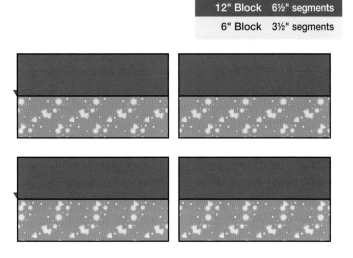

Sewing Block Together

1. Lay out all pieces for block.

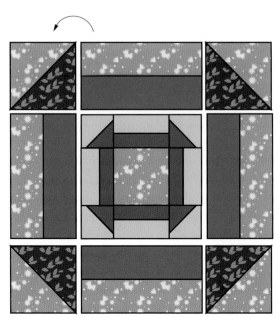

44

2. Flip middle row over row on left.
   Assembly-line sew.

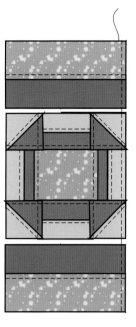

3. Open and assembly-line sew
   row on right.

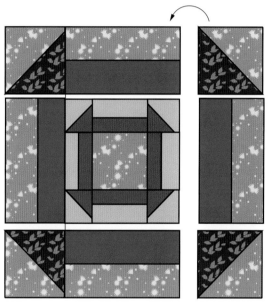

4. Sew remaining rows together, pressing seams
   toward Side Strips.

5. Press last seams away from Inner Wrench.

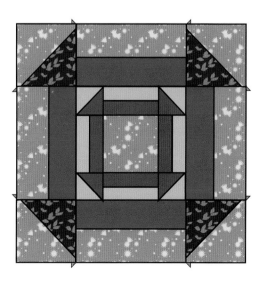

Wagon Wheel

The Wagon Wheel was the second quilt to be displayed on the fence. Wagons with hidden compartments were one of the primary means of transporting escaping runaways.

The quilt was a message to pack provisions for their journey as if they were packing a wagon. Considering limited space and weight, they should pack supplies that would be essential for survival.

The wagon was also symbolic of a "chariot that was to carry them home." The spirituals they sang carried hidden messages, as *Swing Low, Sweet Chariot.*

Sunbonnets and bandannas were indicators of social rank for women. Bonnets were worn by women above the rank of slave and indentured servants. But a sunbonnet could help fleeing slaves disguise themselves by obscuring their faces. If a woman was to tilt her head slightly down, with her eyes looking shyly to the ground, she could use a bonnet for disguise.

In Nebraska City, Nebraska, stories still circulate about a minister who used to drive his wagon with two sunbonneted ladies sitting beside him. A half hour later, the minister would return with two ladies still sitting beside him. What no one seemed to notice was that on this return trip, the two women wearing the bonnets had dark complexions.

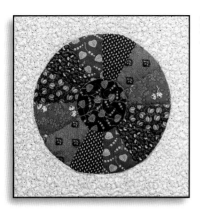

Skill Level
Easy

Tools to Gather
6" x 12" ruler
permanent marking pen
invisible thread
applique foot
stiletto

		12" Finished Size	6" Finished Size
Background #2			
	Background Square	13" square	7" square
Brown #1			
	Spokes	(1) 5" x 6"	(1) 3" x 4"
Blue #2			
	Spokes	(1) 5" x 6"	(1) 3" x 4"
Blue #3			
	Spokes	(1) 5" x 6"	(1) 3" x 4"
Green #1			
	Spokes	(1) 5" x 6"	(1) 3" x 4"
Red #1			
	Spokes	(1) 5" x 6"	(1) 3" x 4"
Red #3			
	Spokes	(1) 5" x 6"	(1) 3" x 4"
Brown #2			
	Center Circle	(1) 5" square	(1) 2½" square
Fusible Interfacing		⅓ yd	¼ yd
Template Plastic		3½" x 5"	3" x 4"

Making the Wagon Wheel Block

1. Trace wedge pattern on template plastic. Cut out shape with all purpose scissors. Patterns are on pages 52-53.

Spoke Wedge

2. On each Spoke fabric, trace and cut two wedges.

12" Block	5" x 6"
6" Block	3" x 4"

3. Place wedges in the order you want them to be sewn. Place two like wedges in each stack. Number stacks.

4. Flip wedges right sides together into pairs, and assembly-line sew.

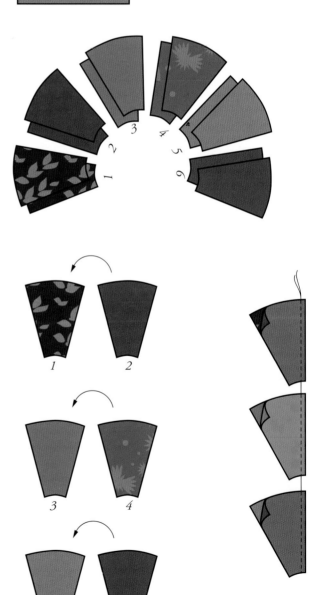

48

5. Set seams and press toward even numbered wedges.

6. Sew pairs right sides together to create half circles. From wrong sides, press seams counter clock wise.

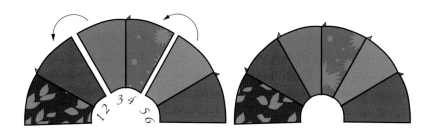

7. Place each half circle on gridded cutting mat. Line up seam between Wedges 3 and 4 on horizontal line. Line up each end of half circle on vertical line. Edges of inner circle should be on line.

8. Sliver trim excess fabric.

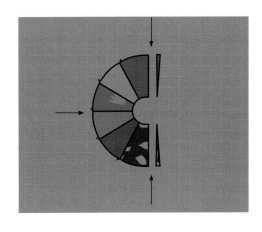

9. Sew two halves right sides together into complete circle. Press seams in same direction.

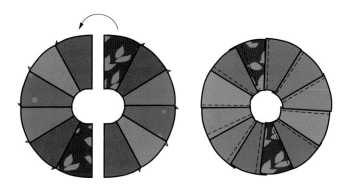

Completing the Circles

1. Place non-woven interfacing smooth side up on Wagon Wheel Pattern for Wedges. Trace with permanent marking pen. Place interfacing on Wagon Wheel Center, and trace. Leave at least 1" between pieces.

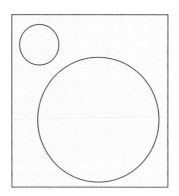

2. Cut apart, leaving at least ½" of interfacing around drawn circles.

3. Place "bumpy" side of small circle interfacing against right side of Center Circle fabric. Pin.

4. Using an applique foot, sew on drawn line with 18-20 stitches per inch. If possible, lighten pressure on your presser foot.

Wheel Center

12" Block	5" square
6" Block	2½" square

5. Trim to ⅛" from seam line.

6. Make a small slit in center of interfacing.

7. Turn right side out with fingers.

8. Run point turner around inside and push out edges. Press with wooden iron.

9. Using same technique, center bumpy side of large circle interfacing on right side of Wedges. Sew from interfacing side.

10. Trim and turn right side out through Wedges.

11. Run point turner around inside and push out edges. Press with wooden iron.

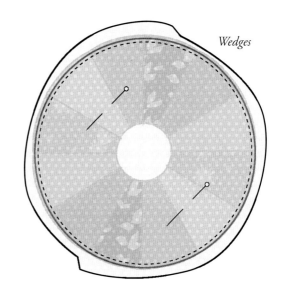

Wedges

Completing the Block

1. Press Background in fourths. Center large and small circles on Background. Fuse in place with steam. Press on wrong side.

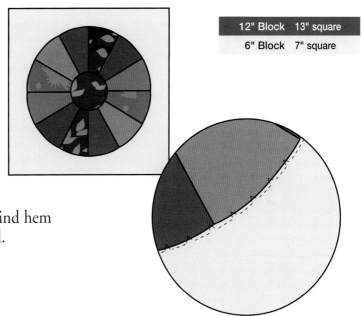

12" Block	13" square
6" Block	7" square

2. Applique in place by machine with blind hem stitch and invisible thread, or by hand.

3. Center Wagon Wheel and square up block.

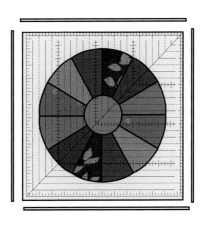

12" Block	12½" square
6" Block	6½" square

Wagon Wheel Patterns

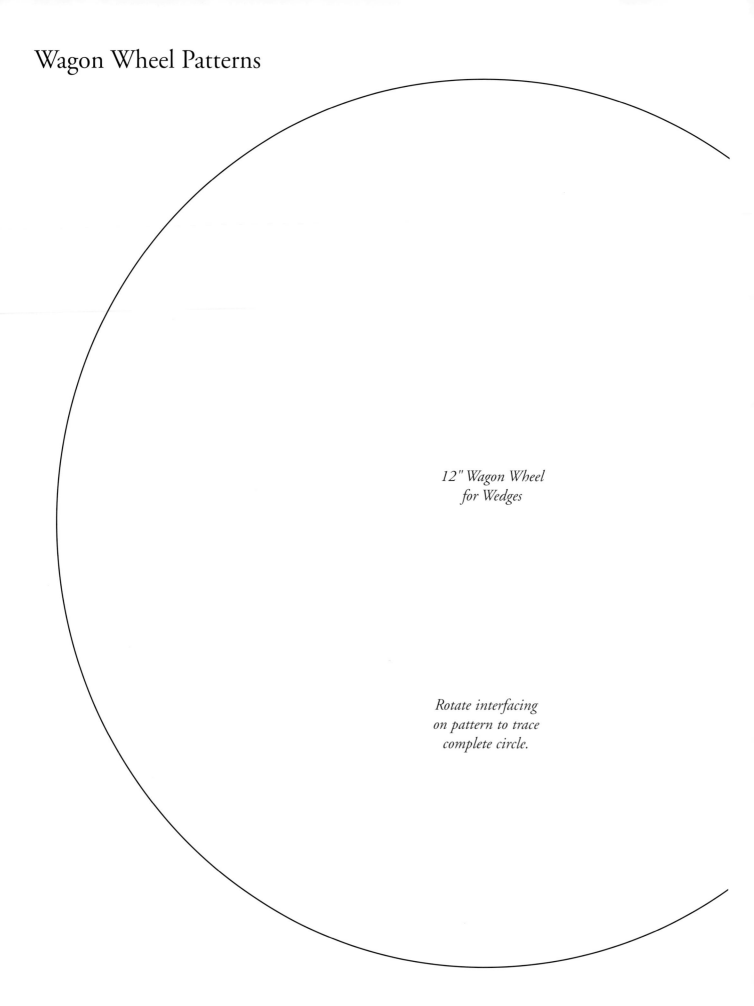

*12" Wagon Wheel
for Wedges*

*Rotate interfacing
on pattern to trace
complete circle.*

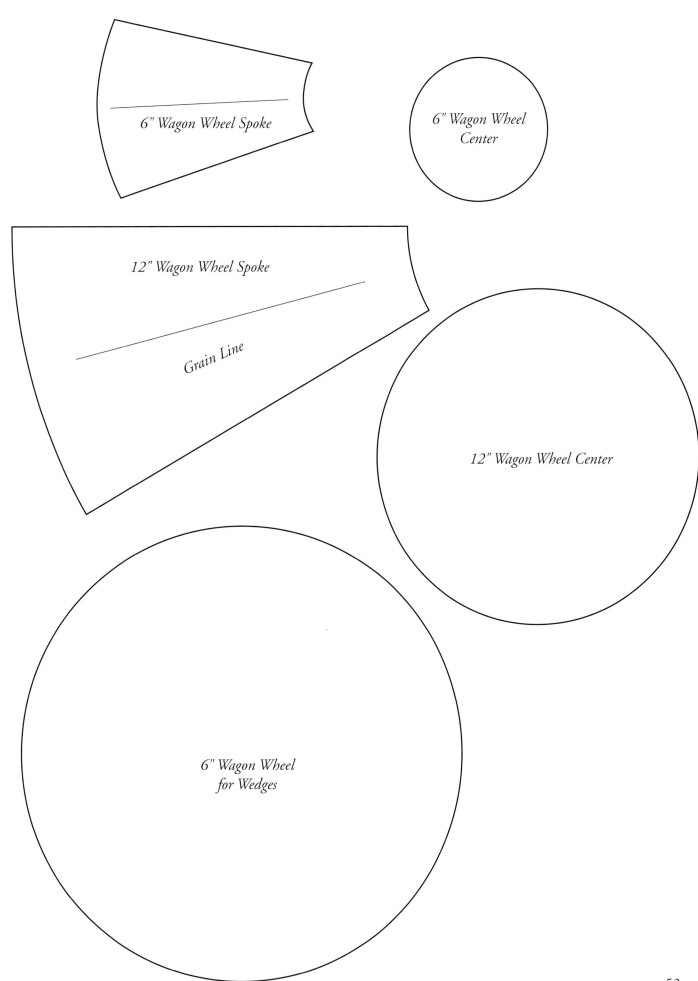

6" Wagon Wheel Spoke

6" Wagon Wheel
Center

12" Wagon Wheel Spoke

Grain Line

12" Wagon Wheel Center

6" Wagon Wheel
for Wedges

Carpenter's Wheel

The Carpenter's Wheel Quilt was a secondary code pattern, as explained by Ozella Williams to Jacqueline Tobin, author of Hidden in Plain View. To a slave, the master carpenter in their lives was Jesus. As they worked in the fields, they sang this well-known spiritual about a chariot that was to carry them home.

> *Swing Low, Sweet Chariot*
> *Comin' for to carry me home.*
> *If you get a dere befo I do,*
> *Tell all my friends I'm comin too.*

Plantation owners thought they were singing about joining Jesus in Heaven, but the song held hidden messages! Future run-aways recognized this as a directive to plan their escape. They were to follow the Carpenter's Wheel to the west-northwest. Imagine the beauty of the sun setting behind the Appalachian mountains to the west on their journey to Ohio and freedom.

Skill Level
Intermediate

Tools to Gather
6" x 12" ruler
6½" Triangle Square Up ruler
Small 3" x 6" Flying Geese Ruler
6" Square Up ruler
permanent marking pen
stiletto

	12" Finished Size	6" Finished Size
Background #3		
Wheel Rim and Corners	(8) 2" squares	(8) 1¼" squares
Sides	(4) 2" x 3½"	(4) 1¼" x 2"
Star Points and Flying Geese	(4) 3½" squares	(4) 2" squares
Flying Geese	(2) 4½" squares	(8) 1¼" x 2"
Blue #1		
Flying Geese	(2) 6" squares	(16) 1¼" squares
Wheel Rim Rectangle	(4) 2" x 3½"	(4) 1¼" x 2"
Flying Geese	(8) 2" squares	(8) 1¼" squares
Wheel Rim	(4) 2" squares	(4) 1¼" squares
Red #2		
Star Center	(1) 2½" x 5"	(1) 2" x 4"
Star Points	(4) 2" squares	(4) 1¼" squares
Blue #3		
Star Center	(1) 2½" x 5"	(1) 2" x 4"
Star Points	(4) 2" squares	(4) 1¼" squares

Carpenter's Wheel Sections

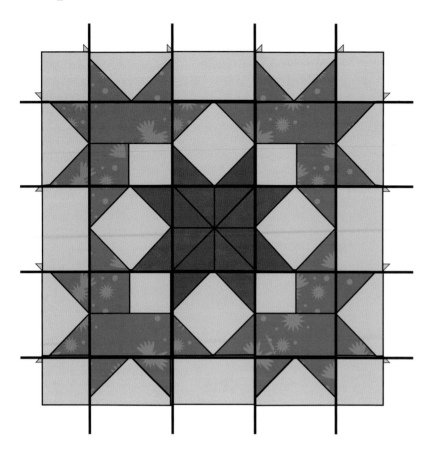

1 Star Center

12" Block	3½" square
6" Block	2" square

4 Star Points and Flying Geese

12" Block	3½" square
6" Block	2" square

8 Flying Geese

12" Block	2" x 3½"
6" Block	2" x 1¼"

4 Wheel Rims

12" Block	3½" square
6" Block	2" square

Making One Star Center

1. Place one Star Center rectangle right sides together to second Star Center rectangle.

12" Block	2½" x 5"
6" Block	2" x 4"

2. Place on gridded cutting mat. Draw center line and one diagonal line in each square.

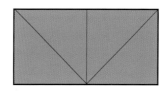

12" Block	2½" squares
6" Block	2" squares

3. Sew ¼" from both sides of diagonal lines. Set seams.

4. Cut apart on all drawn lines.

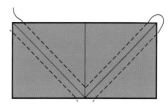

5. Square up patches with 6½" Triangle Square Up ruler. Clip corners. Press seams toward blue Star fabric.

12" Block	2" square
6" Block	1¼" square

6. Lay out four patches to form Star Center. Pay attention to fabric color arrangement. Flip piece on right over piece on left.

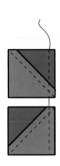

Red Star

Blue Star

7. Assembly-line sew.

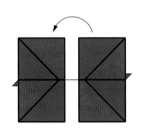

8. Open, and flip right sides together. Lock top seam up and underneath seam down. Sew Star Center together.

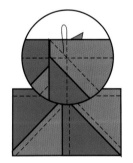
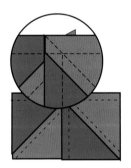

9. At center seam, cut first stitch with scissors. See circle.

10. Remove three straight stitches on both sides with stiletto or seam ripper.

11. Open center seams and push flat to form a tiny pinwheel.

12. Press seams clockwise around block.

13. Measure.

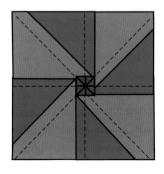
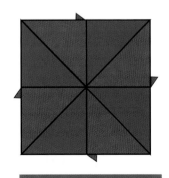

| 12" Block | 3½" square |
| 6" Block | 2" square |

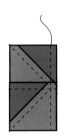

Making Four Star Points and Flying Geese

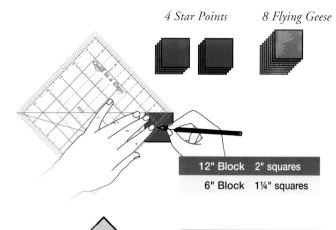

4 Star Points   *8 Flying Geese*

1. Draw diagonal lines on wrong sides of four red Star Point squares, four blue Star Point squares, and eight blue Flying Geese squares.

    Optional: If available, use Angler in place of drawing diagonal lines.

12" Block	2" squares
6" Block	1¼" squares

2. Place red Star Point right sides together to corner of Background square. Use center needle position and open toe applique foot. Assembly-line sew on right side of drawn lines.

12" Block	3½" square
6" Block	2" square

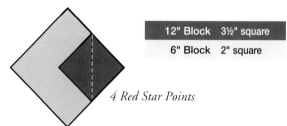

4 Red Star Points

3. Count out four squares from stack of Flying Geese. On opposite corner, place a Flying Geese square. Assembly-line sew on right side of drawn lines.

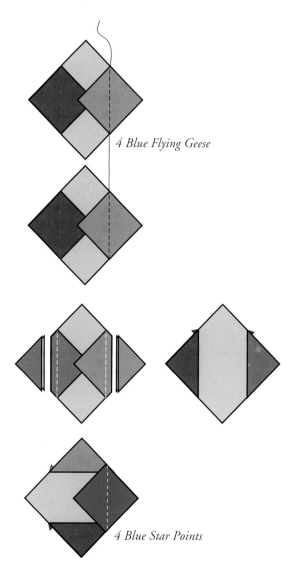

4 Blue Flying Geese

4. Set seams. Trim ¼" from sewn lines. Press seams away from Background.

5. Place blue Star Point right sides together to corner of Background square. Assembly-line sew on right side of drawn lines.

4 Blue Star Points

6. On opposite side, place remaining four Flying Geese squares. Assembly-line sew on right side drawn lines.

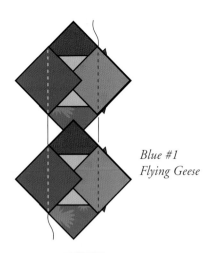

*Blue #1
Flying Geese*

7. Set seams. Trim ¼" from sewn lines. Press seams away from Background.

8. Measure.

Star Points 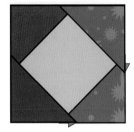 *Flying Geese*

Making Four Wheel Rims

1. Sew four Wheel Rim squares to four Background squares. Press seams toward Wheel Rim fabric.

12" Block	2" squares
6" Block	1¼" squares

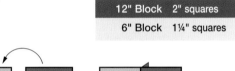
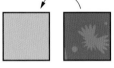

2. Sew patch right sides together to Wheel Rim Rectangle.

12" Block	2" x 3½"
6" Block	1¼" x 2"

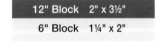
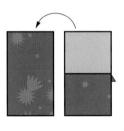

3. Set seams and press toward rectangle.

4. Measure.

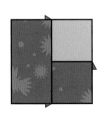

12" Block	3½" squares
6" Block	2" squares

▽ Making Eight Flying Geese for 12" Block

1. Place 4½" Background squares right sides together and centered on 6" Geese squares. Draw diagonal lines on wrong sides of Background squares.

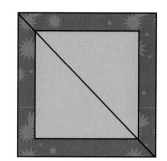

2. Follow instructions for making Flying Geese on pages 28-31. Use the Small Flying Geese ruler and square up to 2" x 3½". Finished size is 1½" x 3".

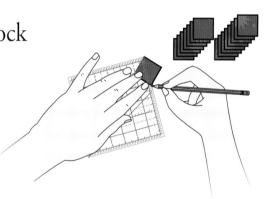

Making Eight Flying Geese for 6" Block

1. Draw diagonal lines on wrong sides of sixteen 1¼" Flying Geese squares.

   Optional: If available, use Angler in place of drawing diagonal lines.

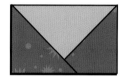

2. Place 1¼" Flying Geese square right sides together to 1¼" x 2" Background. Sew on drawn lines.

3. Trim ¼" from line. Press seam toward Geese.

4. Repeat on remaining side.

Completing the Block

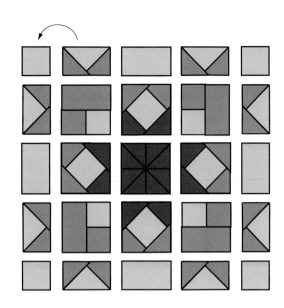

1. Lay out all pieces for block.

   If individual pieces measure less than indicated, sew together with scant ¼" seam.

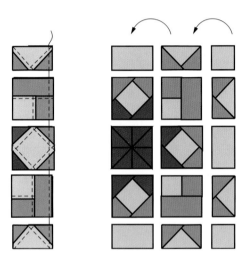

2. Flip second vertical row to first vertical row. Assembly-line sew.

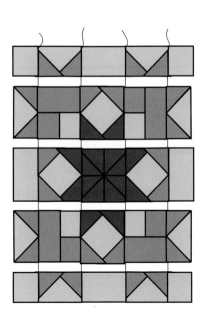

3. Open and continue to sew vertical rows together.

4. Press seams away from Flying Geese patches and Star Point/Flying Geese patches.

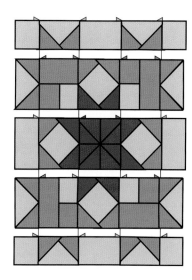

5. Turn and sew remaining rows together.

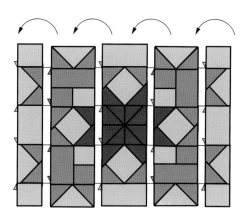

6. Set seams. Press last seams away from center row.

Bear's Paw

The Bear's Paw Quilt, according to the family history of Ozella McDaniel Williams, was the third quilt used to help prepare slaves for their journey to freedom.

Runaways were directed to follow the actual trail of a bear's footprints. Animal footprints would indicate the best path, just like a road map, through the mountains. Following the bear's paws would also lead tired, hungry runaways to food and water.

Reference has been given specifically to the Appalachian mountain range, closest to the South Carolina area and plantations owned by slave holders. The range ran southwest to northeast that paralleled the Underground Railroad route. Most certainly, there were bears in these mountains, roaming about and searching for food after their long winter hibernation. Most escapes took place in the spring. With spring rains, it would be easy to follow a bear's paw trail to food and safety!

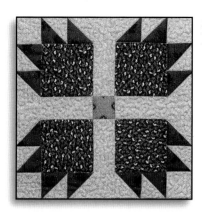

Skill Level
Intermediate

Tools to Gather
6" x 12" ruler
6½" Triangle Square Up ruler
permanent marking pen
stiletto

	12" Finished Size	6" Finished Size
Background #4		
Corners	(4) 2¼" squares	(4) 1⅜" squares
Dividing Strips	(4) 2" x 5¾"	(4) 1¼" x 3⅛"
Claws	(2) 6" squares	(2) 4" squares
Green #3		
Claws	(2) 6" squares	(2) 4" squares
Red #3		
Paws	(4) 4" squares	(4) 2¼" squares
Blue #1		
Center	(1) 2" square	(1) 1¼" square

Making Bear's Claws

1. Place Background squares right sides together to Claw squares. Draw diagonal lines on wrong sides of Background squares.

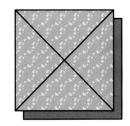

12" Block	6" squares
6" Block	4" squares

2. Set up machine with thread that shows against wrong side of both fabrics. It is important to see the stitching.

3. Sew exactly ¼" from lines with 15 stitches to the inch or a setting of #2.

4. Press to set seams.

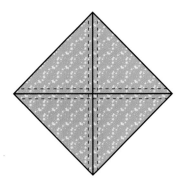

5. Without moving fabric, cut squares horizontally and vertically.

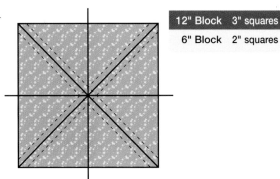

12" Block	3" squares
6" Block	2" squares

6. Cut on both diagonal lines. There should be a total of sixteen closed triangles.

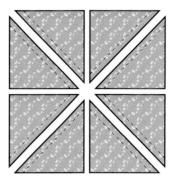

7. Square up with Triangle Square Up ruler. Press seams toward Claw.

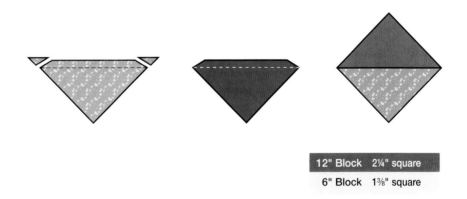

| 12" Block | 2¼" square |
| 6" Block | 1⅜" square |

Making the Paws

1. Make four stacks with four in each. Turn two stacks in one direction. Turn two stacks in a second direction.

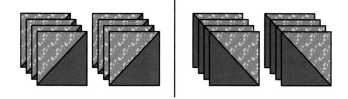

2. Select first two stacks. Flip piece on right to piece on left. Assembly-line sew patches together.

   Use stiletto to help feed pieces and match edges.

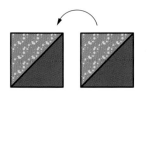

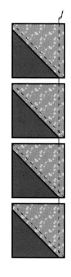

3. Turn over, and drop on pressing mat with stitches **across bottom.** Set seams. Open and press flat. Clip apart.

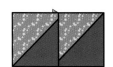

Seam is pressed to left.

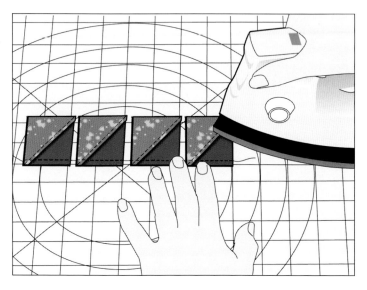

4. Check the placement of diagonal seams on remaining two stacks of Claws.

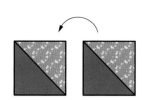

5. Assembly-line sew patches together.

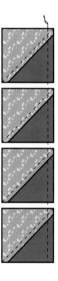

6. Drop on pressing mat with stitches **across top**. Set seams. Open and press flat. Clip apart.

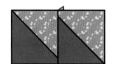

Seam is pressed to right.

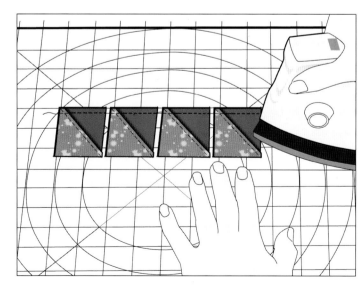

7. Lay out Paws with Claws and Background square. You should have four pieces in each stack.

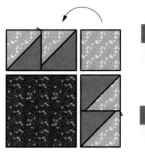

12" Block	2¼" square
6" Block	1⅜" square

12" Block	4" paw
6" Block	2¼" paw

8. Flip Background square right sides together to two Claws and sew.

9. Flip two Claws right sides together to Paw and assembly-line sew, alternating between two, until all pieces have been sewn together.

10. Clip threads every two pieces.

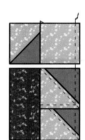

11. Turn and flip right sides together. Finger press seams on top toward Background, and seams underneath toward Paw. Lock seams.

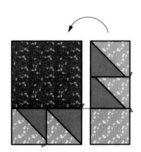

12. Assembly-line sew all Paws.

13. Press last seam toward Paw.

14. Measure Paw.

12" Block	5¾" squares
6" Block	3⅛" squares

Completing the Bear's Paw Block

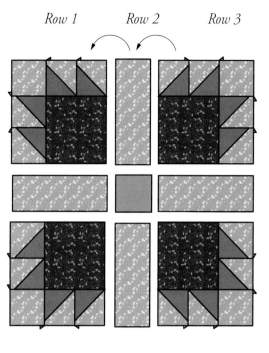

Row 1   *Row 2*   *Row 3*

1. Lay out all pieces.

2. Flip middle vertical row onto first row. Assembly-line sew. Flip third row onto middle row. Assembly-line sew. Press seams toward Background.

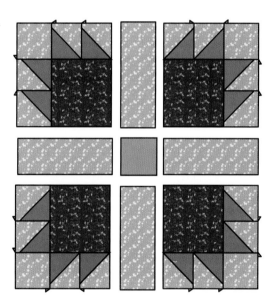

3. Sew center rows together. Press seams toward Background.

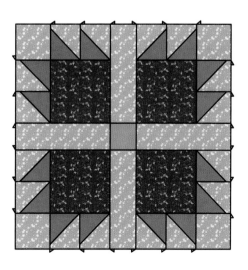

Basket

The Basket Block is a symbol of the provisions needed for the long journey North.

One of the most difficult things faced by escaping slaves was feeding themselves along the journey. They took what provisions they could carry, instructed to pack as if they were packing a wagon. Since they had to keep themselves secret, they couldn't walk into most towns and buy food. They often depended on safe houses or friends along the way. Abolitionists would give them baskets of provisions and tools, such as flint and compasses, to aid them in their flight.

One of the ways the provisions were carried was in a laundry or sewing basket. A story is told about a woman who had a safe house where she hid escapees upstairs. She would carry her laundry basket up and down the stairs, filled with food. A woman carrying a full laundry basket wouldn't arouse suspicion, even if the clothes hid important supplies. She could transport food to her charges, looking for all the world like an ordinary woman going about her work.

Skill Level
Easy

Tools to Gather
6" x 12" ruler
6½" Triangle Square Up ruler
permanent marking pen
stiletto

		12" Finished Size	6" Finished Size
Background #1			
	Handle	(1) 8" square	(1) 5" square
	Sides	(2) 3½" x 6½"	(2) 2" x 3½"
	Bottom	(1) 7" square	(1) 4" square
Blue #1			
	Base	(1) 3½" square	(1) 2" square
Blue #2			
	Handle	(1) 8" square	(1) 5" square
	Feet	(1) 4" square	(1) 2½" square

Making the Handle and Basket

1. Place Background Handle square right sides together to Dark Handle square. Draw an X.

12" Block	8" squares
6" Block	5" squares

2. Sew ¼" from both sides of diagonal lines with slightly contrasting thread. Set seams.

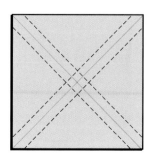

3. Cut into squares. Cut on drawn diagonal lines so you have eight triangles.

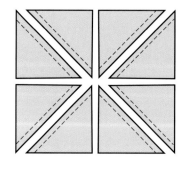

12" Block	4" squares
6" Block	2½" squares

4. Square up patches with Triangle Square-Up ruler. Clip corners. Press seams toward dark.

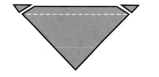 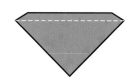

12" Block	3½" square
6" Block	2" square

5. Lay out with Base.

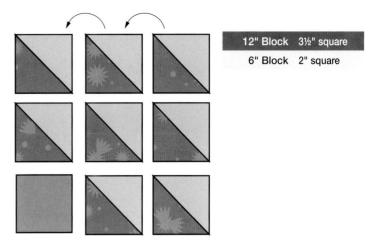

12" Block	3½" square
6" Block	2" square

6. Flip middle vertical row over row on left. Assembly-line sew.

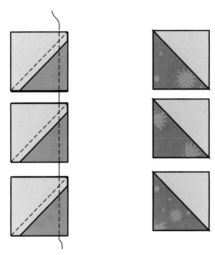

7. Repeat with remaining row. Press Rows One and Three to right. Press Row Two to left.

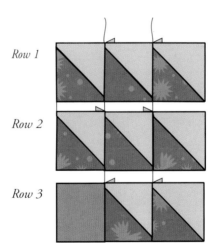

Row 1

Row 2

Row 3

8. Sew rows together. From Base, press seams in same direction.

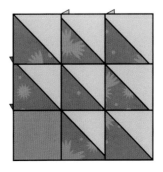

Finishing the Basket

1. Cut Feet in half on one diagonal. Sew Feet to ends of Side pieces. They are mirror image.

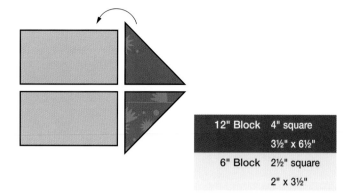

12" Block	4" square
	3½" x 6½"
6" Block	2½" square
	2" x 3½"

2. Press seams toward Basket Feet.

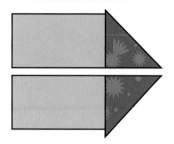

3. Lock seam, and sew one Foot to right side of Basket.

4. Press seam away from Basket.

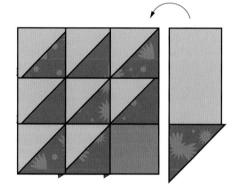

5. Sew remaining Foot to left side of Basket.

6. Press seam away from Basket.

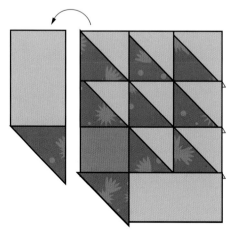

7. Trim off bottom, leaving a ¼" seam from Basket Base.

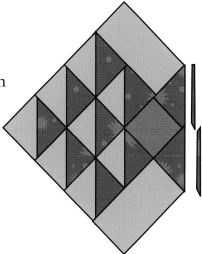

8. Cut Bottom square in half on one diagonal.

12" Block	7" square
6" Block	4" square

9. Sew one triangle to bottom of Basket. Press seam away from Basket. One triangle is extra.

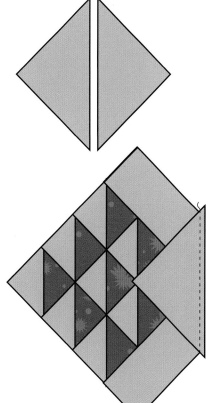

10. Trim excess Background from base of Basket.

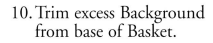
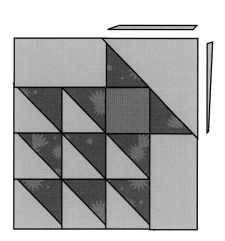

Crossroads

The Crossroads Quilt was the fourth quilt with symbolic meaning revealed to slaves planning to escape.

Once fugitives made it safely through the Appalachian Mountains, they were to travel to the "crossroads," or a city where they would find protection and refuge. The main crossroads or terminal was Cleveland, Ohio. Four or five overland trails connected with Cleveland, and numerous water routes, crossing Lake Erie into Canada and freedom.

As part of their secret language, fugitives referred to Cleveland as Hope. Detroit, Michigan was another "crossroads" referred to as Midnight. Men ready to be delivered to safety were "hardware," and women were "dry goods."

The first four blocks make up a directive code for men and women headed for freedom!

"The Monkey wrench turns the wagon wheel toward Canada on a bear's paw trail to the crossroads."

Skill Level
Easy

	12" Finished Size	6" Finished Size
Background #1		
Side Triangles	(3) 5½" squares	(3) 3½" squares
Crossroads	(9) 2½" squares	(9) 1½" squares
Corners	(2) 3½" squares	(2) 2" squares
Red #1		
Crossroads	(16) 2½" squares	(16) 1½" squares

Making Crossroads Block

1. Cut three Background squares on both diagonals for Side Triangles.

12" Block	5½" squares
6" Block	3½" squares

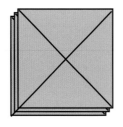 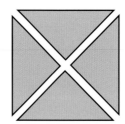

2. Count out four Red and three Background squares, alternating colors. Lay out Row 4. Assembly-line sew together. Press seams toward red.

12" Block	2½" squares
6" Block	1½" squares

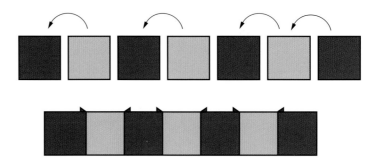

3. Stack two pieces each in remaining Rows.

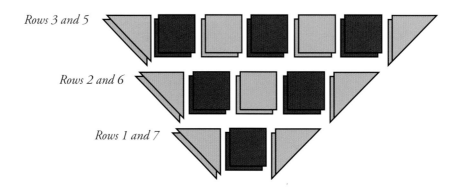

Rows 3 and 5

Rows 2 and 6

Rows 1 and 7

4. Sew two identical rows at a time, matching square corners, and tips on Side Triangles extending.

Rows 1 and 7

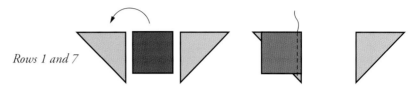

5. Press seams toward Crossroads.

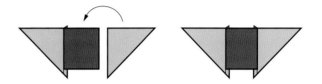

6. Trim excess tips from Side Triangles.

Rows 2 and 6

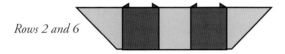

7. Sew rows together, locking seams.

Row 1

Row 2

Row 3

Row 4

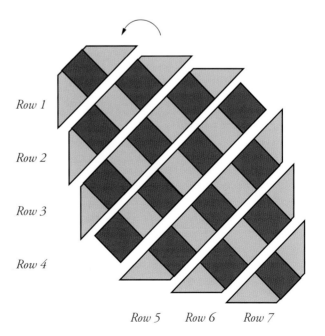

Row 5   *Row 6*   *Row 7*

8. Press seams away from middle row.

View from the back.

9. Cut two Background squares on one diagonal.

12" Block	3½" squares
6" Block	2" squares

10. Sew one triangle to each corner.

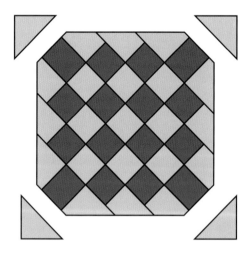

11. Square up block using a 12½" Square Up ruler or 6½" Triangle Square Up ruler.

82

68" x 98"   *Lori Forsythe*

Inspiration for fabric selection came from the beautiful floral border. Lori brought in more than the suggested thirteen colors for bigger variety in color combinations.

Log Cabin

The log cabin block is the fifth quilt in the secret code as revealed by Ozella McDaniel Williams.

The block may have indicated there was a specific log cabin in Cleveland that was a safe house. Research did not uncover it, but after all it was a long time ago, and it may have deteriorated.

It also may have directed runaways to build a log cabin to weather out winter and establish permanent residency in a "free" area.

The usual center color of the block was red, representing the hearth or fire of the cabin.

Gladys-Marie Fry, in *Stitched from the Soul*, suggested a log cabin quilt with a black center hanging in front of a house indicated it was a "safe" house.

A yellow center indicated a light or beacon in the wilderness. William Lloyd Still, famous black Underground Railroad conductor, had a Log Cabin quilt with a yellow center in his Philadelphia family home.

Skill Level
Easy

Each light is used twice in block. Each dark is used only once.

Tools to Gather
12½" Square Up ruler

8 squares at 12" ea
Lights - 8 strips each size for 16 in all
Darks - 8 strips ea

Fabric	Piece	12" Finished Size	6" Finished Size
Black	Center	2½" square	1½" square
Background #2	1st Light	1¾" x 2½" 1¾" x 3¾"	1⅛" x 1½" 1⅛" x 2⅛"
Background #1	2nd Light	1¾" x 5" 1¾" x 6¼"	1⅛" x 2¾" 1⅛" x 3⅜"
Background #3	3rd Light	1¾" x 7½" 1¾" x 8¾"	1⅛" x 4" 1⅛" x 4⅝"
Background #4	4th Light	2" x 10" 2" x 11¼"	1⅜" x 5¼" 1⅜" x 6⅛"
Blue #1	1st Dark	1¾" x 3¾"	1⅛" x 2⅛"
Red #3	2nd Dark	1¾" x 5"	1⅛" x 2¾"
Red #2	3rd Dark	1¾" x 6¼"	1⅛" x 3⅜"
Red #1	4th Dark	1¾" x 7½"	1⅛" x 4"
Green #1	5th Dark	1¾" x 8¾"	1⅛" x 4⅝"
Blue #2	6th Dark	1¾" x 10"	1⅛" x 5¼"
Brown #2	7th Dark	2" x 11¼"	1⅜" x 6⅛"
Brown #1	8th Dark	2" x 13"	1⅜" x 7"

Making the Log Cabin Block

1. Lay out all pieces in sewing order.

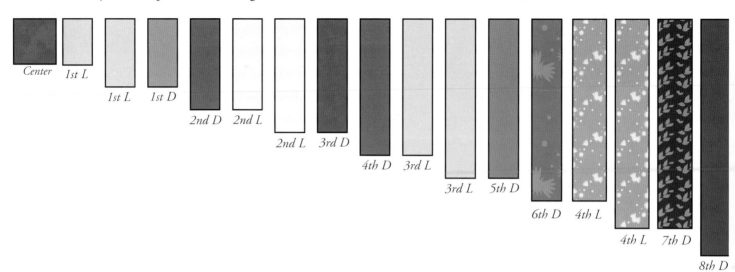

2. Flip Center Square right sides together to First Light, and sew. Finger press seam away from Center Square.

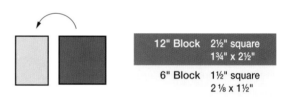

12" Block	2½" square
	1¾" x 2½"
6" Block	1½" square
	2 ⅛ x 1½"

3. Flip patch to remaining 1st Light, and sew. Finger press seam away from Center patch.

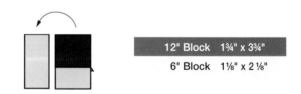

12" Block	1¾" x 3¾"
6" Block	1⅛" x 2⅛"

4. Flip patch to 1st Dark, and sew. Finger press seam away from Center.

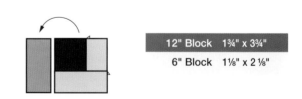

12" Block	1¾" x 3¾"
6" Block	1⅛" x 2⅛"

5. Flip patch to 2nd Dark, and sew. Finger press seam away from Center.

12" Block	1¾" x 5"
6" Block	1⅛" x 2¾"

6. Flip patch to 2nd Light, and sew. Finger press seam away from Center.

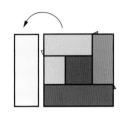

12" Block	1¾" x 5"
6" Block	1⅛" x 2¾"

7. Flip patch to remaining 2nd Light, and sew. Finger press seam away from Center.

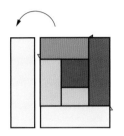

12" Block	1¾" x 6¼"
6" Block	1⅛" x 3⅜"

8. Flip patch to 3rd Dark, and sew. Finger press seam away from Center.

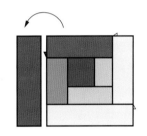

12" Block	1¾" x 6¼",
6" Block	1⅛" x 3⅜"

9. Flip patch to 4th Dark, and sew. Finger press seam away from Center.

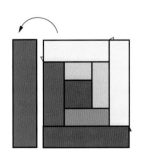

12" Block	1¾" x 7½"
6" Block	1⅛" x 4"

10. Flip patch to 3rd Light, and sew. Finger press seam away from Center.

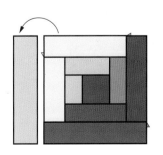

12" Block	1¾" x 7½"
6" Block	1⅛" x 4"

11. Flip patch to remaining 3rd Light, and sew. Finger press seam away from Center.

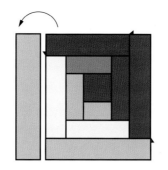

12" Block	1¾" x 8¾"
6" Block	1⅛" x 4⅝"

12. Flip patch to 5th Dark, and sew. Finger press seam away from Center.

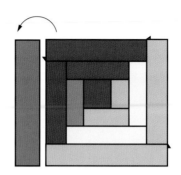

12" Block	1¾" x 8¾"
6" Block	1⅛" x 4⅝"

13. Flip patch to 6th Dark, and sew. Finger press seam away from Center.

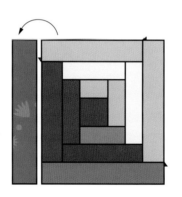

12" Block	1¾" x 10"
6" Block	1⅛" x 5¼"

14. Flip patch to 4th Light, and sew. Finger press seam away from Center.

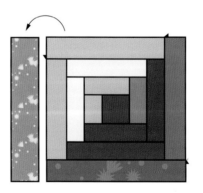

12" Block	2" x 10"
6" Block	1⅜" x 5¼"

15. Flip patch to remaining 4th Light, and sew. Finger press seam away from Center.

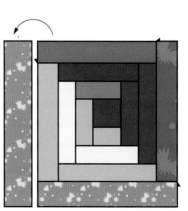

12" Block	2" x 11¼"
6" Block	1⅜" x 6⅛"

16. Flip patch to 7th Dark, and sew. Finger press seam away from Center.

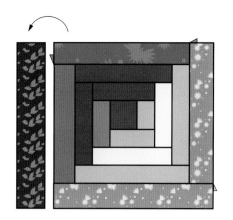

12" Block	2" x 11¼"
6" Block	1⅜" x 6⅛"

17. Flip patch to 8th Dark, and sew. Finger press seam away from Center.

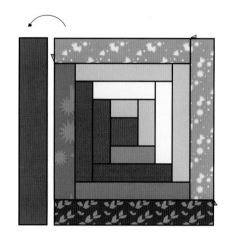

12" Block	2" x 13"
6" Block	1⅜" x 7"

18. Square up block. Trim equally off four sides.

12" Block	12½" square
6" Block	6½" square

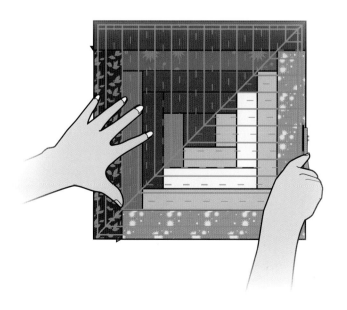

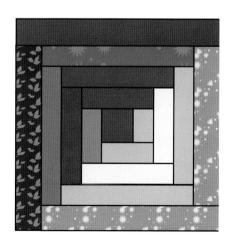

Shoo-Fly

The shoofly represents an actual person who might have helped escaping slaves. His responsibility was to secretly aid and harbor fugitives. Sometimes the slaves hid out in churches, or caves referred to as cathedrals.

Graveyards were frequently the hiding place, especially if they were located on the outskirts of town, or were close to rivers. They may have secretly hid behind gravestones, waiting for a signal from a lantern across town.

The song Steal Away is a directive to run away to freedom. These are the words to that song, with their meaning.

Steal away, steal away.
Steal away to Jesus.

A directive to run away to freedom

Steal away, steal away,
I ain't got long to stay here.

My Lord calls me.
He calls me by the thunder.

Leave in a rainstorm so the dogs won't have a scent to pick up, and footprints will wash away.

Green trees are bending,
poor sinner stands a trembling.

Leave in the summer.

Tombstones are bursting,
poor sinner stands a trembling.

Hide in a graveyard.

My Lord calls me.
He calls me by the lighting.

Lighting will illuminate the landscape.

The trumpet sounds within my soul,
I ain't got long to stay here.

Trumpet and Freedom.

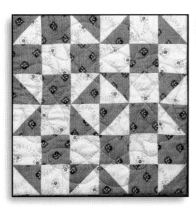

Skill Level
Easy

Tools to Gather
6" x 12" ruler
6½" Triangle Square Up ruler
permanent marking pen
stiletto

	12" Finished Size	6" Finished Size
Background #3		
Triangles	(2) 6" squares	(2) 4" squares
Squares	(10) 2½" squares	(10) 1½" squares
Green #1		
Triangles	(2) 6" squares	(2) 4" squares
Squares	(10) 2½" squares	(10) 1½" squares

Making 16 Triangle Pieced Squares

1. Place Triangle fabrics right sides together. Draw diagonal lines on wrong sides of Background squares.

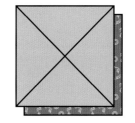

12" Block	6" squares
6" Block	4" squares

2. Set up machine with thread that shows against wrong side of both fabrics. It is important to see the stitching.

3. Sew exactly ¼" from lines with 15 stitches to the inch or a setting of #2.

4. Press to set seams.

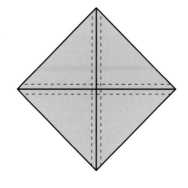

5. Without moving fabric, cut squares horizontally and vertically.

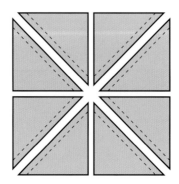

12" Block	3" squares
6" Block	2" squares

6. Cut on both diagonal lines. There should be a total of sixteen closed triangles.

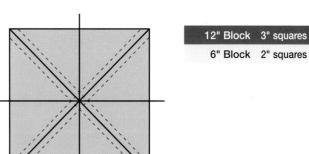

7. Square up with Triangle Square Up ruler. Press seams to dark.

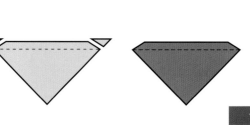

12" Block	2½" square
6" Block	1½" square

Making Two Small Positive Blocks

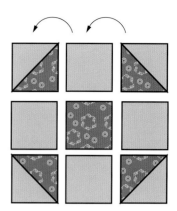

The Shoo Fly block is made from two small positive patches, and two small negative patches.

1. Lay out pieces for two positive blocks.

2. Assembly-line sew vertical rows together.

3. Press seams toward Center square and Triangle Pieced squares.

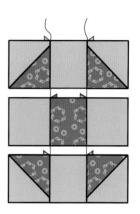

4. Turn and sew remaining rows together.

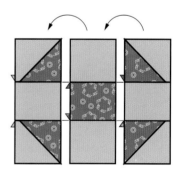

5. Press last seams away from center row.

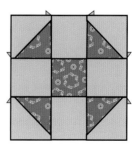

Making Two Small Negative Blocks

1. Lay out pieces for two negative blocks.

2. Assembly-line sew vertical rows together.

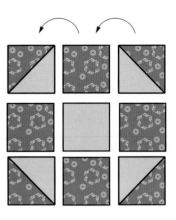

3. Press seams away from Center square and Triangle Pieced squares.

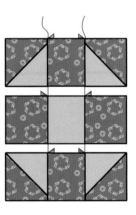

4. Turn and sew remaining rows together.

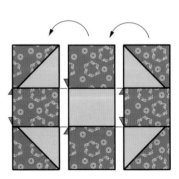

5. Press last seams toward center row.

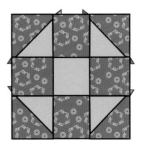

Making One Large Block

1. Measure patches. If they are smaller than desired size, sew patches together with scant ¼" seam.

12" Block	6½" square
6" Block	3½" square

2. Lay out four small blocks, alternating between positive and negative.

3. Sew blocks together, locking seams.

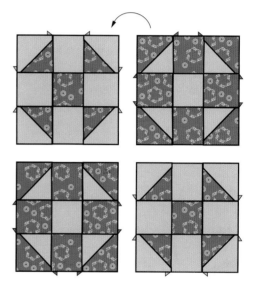

4. Press last seams toward negative blocks.

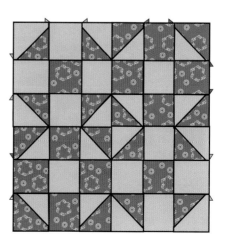

Bow Tie

The Bow Tie Quilt was the seventh quilt displayed on the fence to teach slaves how to escape to freedom. It was a directive for them to dress in a formal manner.

When slaves first escaped, they wore distinguishable garments that eventually became tattered and torn along their journey. Free blacks would often meet them in a safe place as a church, and give them fresh clothing. In "satin bow ties", runaways wouldn't stand out among the city folks.

On the final leg of their journey, slaves could walk through town undetected to ships waiting to take them across the Great Lakes to Canada and freedom.

The triangular quadrants on the Bow Tie block indicate morning, midday, evening, and night. It's also known as Broken Dishes. Broken dishes arranged on a grave site is a superstition among Southern African Americans

When the pattern is turned on its side, an hourglass is created, which is a symbol of time well managed. To the African Secret Society, the hourglass implies you are among friends.

Skill Level
Intermediate

Tools to Gather
6" x 12" ruler
6½" Triangle Square Up ruler
permanent marking pen
stiletto

		12" Finished Size	6" Finished Size
Background #2			
	Bow Ties	(5) 5½" squares	(5) 3½" squares
Red #2			
	Bow Ties	(1) 5½" square	(1) 3½" square
Brown #3			
	Bow Ties	(1) 5½" square	(1) 3½" square
Green #1			
	Bow Ties	(1) 5½" square	(1) 3½" square
Green #2			
	Bow Ties	(1) 5½" square	(1) 3½" square
Blue #2			
	Bow Ties	(1) 5½" square	(1) 3½" square

Making Bow Ties

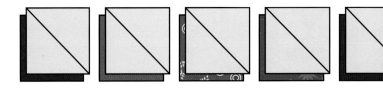

1. Pair five prints and five Background squares right sides together. Draw one diagonal line. Pin.

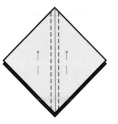

2. Assembly-line sew ¼" from both sides of drawn line.

3. Cut on both diagonals into four pieces.

4. Set seams with dark on top. Open, and press seams toward dark.

5. Lay out two "pairs" of same color triangles so four are in a row. Stack other colors on top.

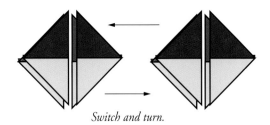

Switch and turn.

6. Switch two center stacks and turn. Sew pairs together with locking seams.

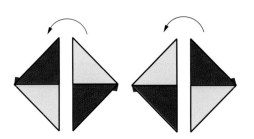

7. Set seams. Do not press open.

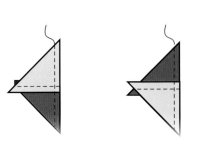

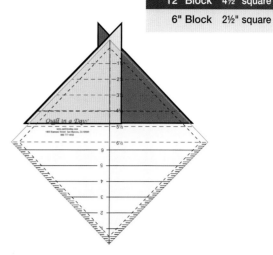

8. Use Triangle Square Up Ruler to square up your patches. Place diagonal line on vertical seam and squaring line on horizontal seam. Trim.

9. Press open.

10. Lay out patches in three rows of three. One patch is extra.

11. Assembly-line sew vertical rows together.

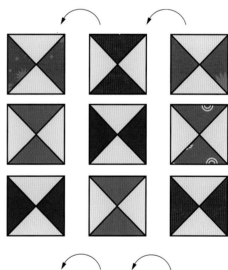

12. Turn and sew remaining rows together, pressing seams in opposite directions.

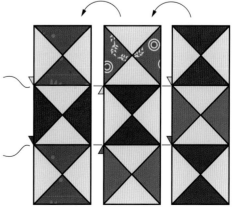

99

Flying Geese

The Flying Geese Quilt is the eighth quilt in the Williams family code.

With the appearance of this quilt, slaves learned they were to take their direction, timing and behavior from migrating geese.

Since geese fly north in the spring, it was also the best time for slaves to escape. Geese have to stop at waterways along their journey in order to rest and eat. Especially since geese make loud honking noises, it was easy for runaways to follow their flight pattern.

The Flying Geese patch is known by several names, including Wild Goose Chase, Dutchman's Puzzle, and Birds in Flight. Geese patches can easily be sewn together in four directions, with two pointing north, two west, two south, and two east in a counter-clockwise movement. A clever quilter wishing to assist the runaways could show direction simply by making one set of Geese distinct from the others.

This one block could act as a compass, transforming the quilt into a map!

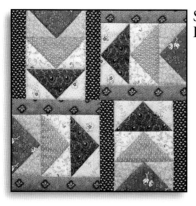

Skill Level
Easy

Tools to Gather
6" x 12" ruler
Large 4" x 8" Flying Geese ruler
permanent marking pen
stiletto

		12" Finished Size	6" Finished Size
Background #1	Sky	(1) 7" square	(8) 1½" squares
Background #3	Sky	(1) 7" square	(8) 1½" squares
Background #4	Sky	(1) 7" square	(8) 1½" squares
Brown #3	Geese	(1) 5½" square	(4) 1½" x 2½"
Green #2	Geese	(1) 5½" square	(4) 1½" x 2½"
Blue #2	Geese	(1) 5½" square	(4) 1½" x 2½"
Red #1	Side Strips	(4) 1½" x 7"	(4) 1" x 4"
Blue #1	Side Strips	(4) 1½" x 7"	(4) 1" x 4"

101

◪ Making Twelve Flying Geese Patches for 12" Block

1. Place three 5½" Geese squares right sides together and centered on three 7" Background squares. Press.

2. Follow instructions for making Flying Geese on pages 28-31.

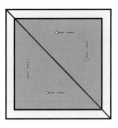

Make 3 sets

3. Place Geese on a small cutting mat so you can rotate the mat as you cut. Use Large 4" x 8" Geese ruler and square up to 2½" x 4½". Finished size is 2" x 4".

4. Line up the ruler's red lines with the 45° sewn lines. Line up the dotted line with the peak of the triangle for the ¼" seam.

5. Cut block in half to separate into two patches, holding ruler firmly.

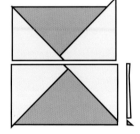

6. Trim off excess fabric on right.

7. Turn patch around. **Do not turn the ruler.** Trim off excess fabric on right and top side.

8. Trim remaining Geese.

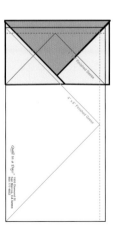

Making Twelve Flying Geese Patches for 6" Block

1. Draw diagonal line on wrong sides of twenty-four 1½" Background squares.

   Optional: If available, use Angler in place of drawing diagonal line.

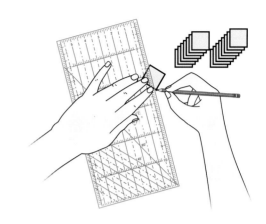

2. Place Background square right sides together to 1½" x 2½" Geese rectangle. Sew on drawn line.

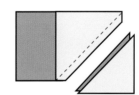 

3. Cut off excess. Press seam toward Background.

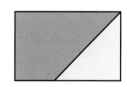

4. Repeat on remaining side.

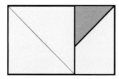 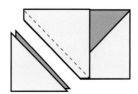 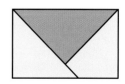

Finishing the Block

1. Place four identical Geese in each stack.

2. Point Flying Geese to the left.

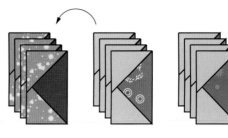

3. Flip middle Geese right sides together to left Geese, and assembly-line sew. Do not clip connecting threads.

4. Flip right Geese right sides together to middle Geese, and assembly-line sew. Clip connecting threads.

5. Press seams toward base of Geese.

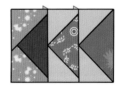

6. Make two stacks of Geese with Side Strips. Sew on Side Strips.

12" Block	1½" x 7"
6" Block	1" x 4"

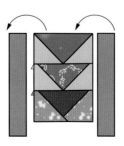

7. Set and press seams toward Side Strips.

8. Square Side Strips even with Geese.

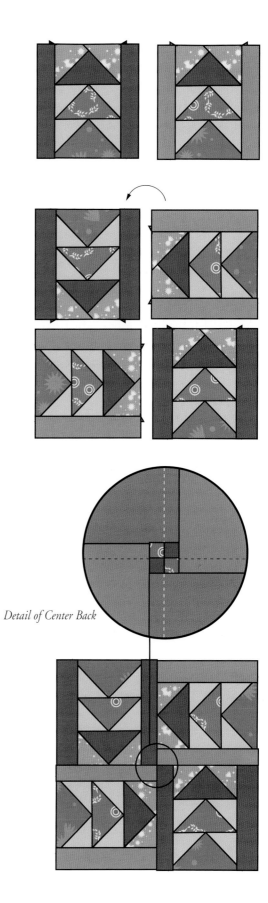

9. Lay out patches and sew together.

10. Unsew stitches in center and press flat into little "Four-Patch." See technique on page 21.

Detail of Center Back

11. Press seams toward Side Strips.

Birds in the Air

The Birds in the Air quilt is symbolic of flight or migration. During the Underground Railroad in the 1840's to 1850's, a clever quilter could indicate a direction for fugitives to travel through the choice of fabric and placement of blocks. In the quilt, notice the blocks in one area are light, creating an arrow pointing North.

A Birds in the Air directional quilt was originally designed by Deborah Coates, wife of Quaker Lindley Coates, of Lancaster County, Pennsylvania. They were abolitionists, and ran Safe House #5 on the Underground Railroad.

According to oral family history, two granddaughters of Deborah could not agree on who should inherit the precious quilt. So, with the Quaker sense of equality, it was decided to cut the quilt exactly in half. When the raw edges were bound over, a small central image of a bound slave was almost totally obscured. Underneath the image were these words: "Deliver me from the oppression of man." When the quilt was passed on to a single descendant, the bindings were opened and the image was brought together again.

That quilt was just one family's way of helping emancipate the slaves!

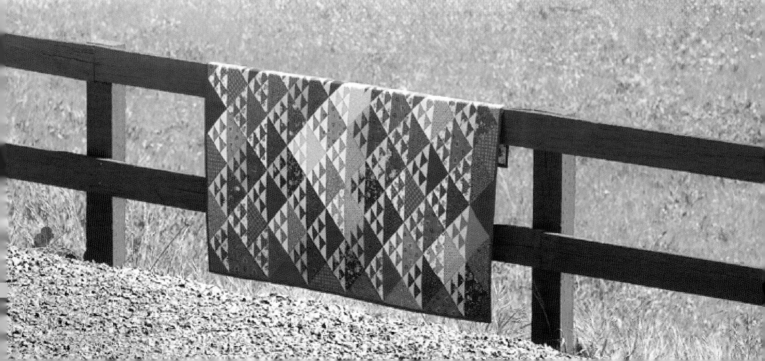

Skill Level
Intermediate

Tools to Gather
6" x 12" ruler
6½" Triangle Square Up ruler
permanent marking pen
stiletto
multi-purpose or open toe presser foot

		12" Finished Size	6" Finished Size
Background #2			
	Sky	(1) 6" square	(1) 4" square
	Sky	(3) 2½" x 3¼"	(3) 1½" x 2¼"
Background #3			
	Sky	(1) 6" square	(1) 4" square
	Sky	(3) 2½" x 3¼"	(3) 1½" x 2¼"
Brown #2			
	Nests	7" x 8"	4" x 5"
Blue #1			
	Nests	7" x 8"	4" x 5"
Red #2			
	Birds	(1) 6" square	(1) 4" square
Green #2			
	Birds	(1) 6" square	(1) 4" square

Making Birds

1. Place two squares of Background and two squares of Birds right sides together. Draw diagonal lines on wrong side of both Background squares. Pin.

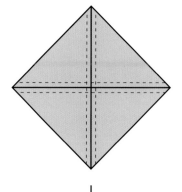

2. Set up machine with thread that shows against wrong side of both fabrics. It is important to see the stitching.

3. Sew exactly ¼" from lines with 15 stitches to the inch or a setting of #2.

4. Press to set seams.

5. Without moving fabric, cut squares horizontally and vertically.

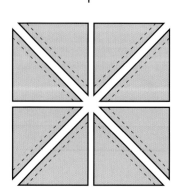

12" Block	3" squares
6" Block	2" squares

6. Cut on both diagonal lines. There should be a total of sixteen closed triangles.

7. Square up with Triangle Square Up ruler. Press seams to dark.

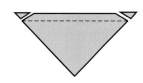  

12" Block	2½" square
6" Block	1½" square

Sewing Birds Together

Birds for two blocks are sewn at the same time.
There are three rows in the Two Block Patch.
Sew only one Two Block Patch at a time.

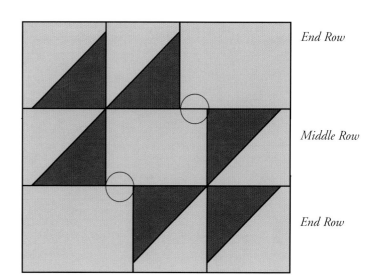

End Row

Middle Row

End Row

Making Two End Rows

1. Place two matching Birds and two matching
   Backgrounds in each stack.

12" Block	2½" x 3¼"
6" Block	1½" x 2¼"

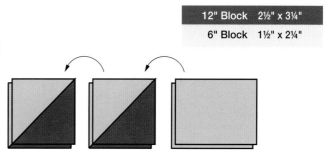

Birds point downward   *Matching Background rectangles*

2. Assembly-line sew right sides together.
3. Press seams away from center patch.

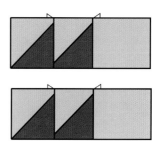

109

Making One Middle Row

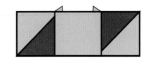

1. Place two matching Birds and one matching Background in this order.

2. Sew right sides together.

3. Press seams toward Background.

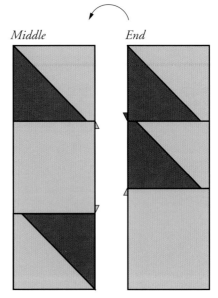

One Middle Row

Sewing Rows Together

1. Lay out Middle Row and one End Row.

2. Flip End Row to Middle Row.

Middle   *End*

Lower seams do not meet.

3. Pin or finger pin top seams so they meet and lock. **The lower seams don't meet.**

4. Be careful that underneath seam does not flip. **Hold seams with stiletto, and sew over seams as pressed.** Match bottom edges.

5. **Finger press.**

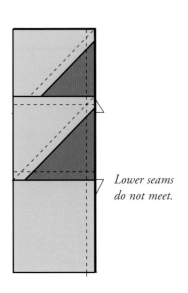

Lower seams do not meet.

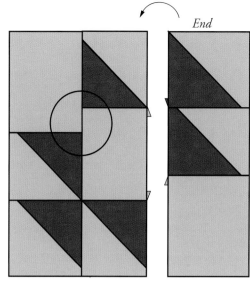

6. On the front, notice in the circle that there is a gap between Birds.

7. Lay out remaining End Row next to Middle Row.

8. Flip End Row to Middle Row. Pin or finger pin top seams so they meet and lock. The lower seams don't meet.

Sew over seams as they were pressed.

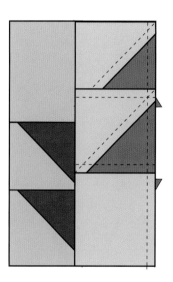

9. **Sew over seams as they were pressed.** Match bottom edges.

10. **On the front**, notice in the circles that there are gaps between Birds.

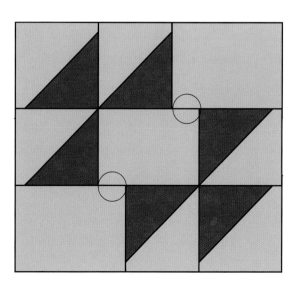

11. **On the wrong side,** use sharp scissors to clip to the stitching in gaps.

12. Press seams on wrong side one half at a time from two Birds toward one Bird. Use a gridded pressing mat to help keep patch straight.

13. Measure your patch.

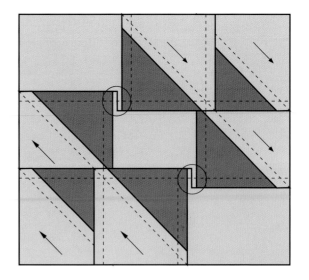

12" Block	6½" x 7¼"
6" Block	3½" x 4¼"

14. Lay patch wrong side up so you can see seams.

15. Line up ruler's 45° line on patch. Shift ruler until its edge touches the "points" of the Birds. See red dots.

Ruler's 45° line

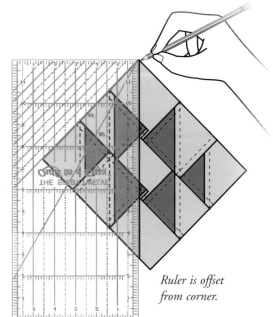

Ruler is offset from corner.

16. Draw a sewing line just to right of "points" from top corner to bottom edge. **Do not cut.**

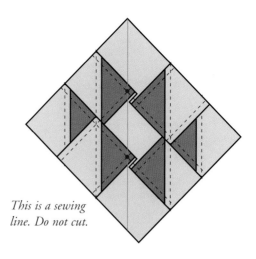

This is a sewing line. Do not cut.

17. Slide ruler over, and repeat match points.

18. **Draw a second sewing line just to left of "points."**

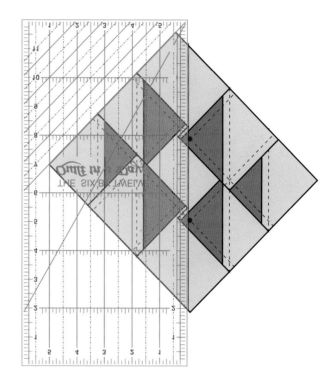

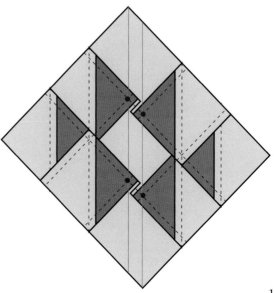

Making Two Block Patches

1. Center marked patch right sides together to Nest. Pin securely. Nest is oversized.

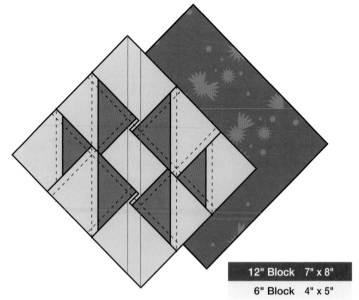

12" Block	7" x 8"
6" Block	4" x 5"

2. **Change to multi-purpose presser foot or open toe foot.**

3. Sew **on** marked line. Use stiletto to hold seams flat.

   If necessary, sew on left side of line so points remain "crisp."

4. Turn around and sew on second marked line.

5. Press on both sides to set seams.

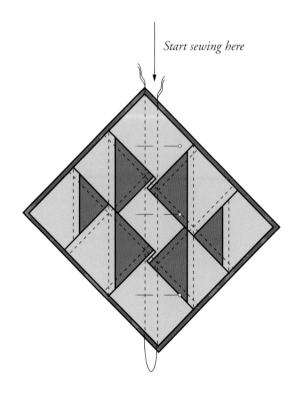

Start sewing here

6. Cut between stitching.

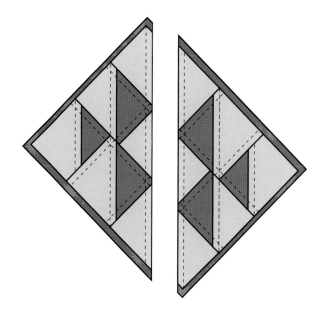

7. Place closed block on pressing mat with Nest side up. Set seam, open, and press seams toward Nest

8. Square up Nest only with 6½" Triangle Square Up ruler.

12" Block	6½" square
6" Block	3½" square

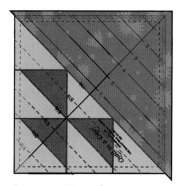

Square up Nest only.

9. If patches are slightly smaller, sew together with scant ¼" seam.

10. Lay out four patches and sew together, pressing center seams in opposite directions.

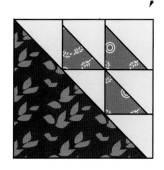
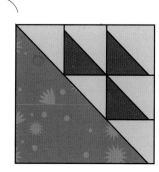
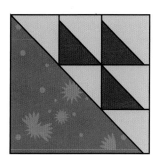
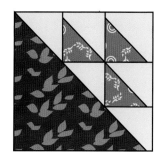

Drunkard's Path

The Drunkard's Path Quilt is the ninth pattern of the secret code.

Slaves were to move in a staggering fashion to allude any following slave hunters. They were to even double back occasionally on their tracks to confuse slave catchers who were pursuing them.

The Underground Railroad got its name from such a pursuit. A Kentucky slave known as Tice was escaping to freedom. He made it to the shore of the Ohio River, near the home of John Rankin's safe house. The slave holder was tracking right behind him! There was no boat tied up for Tice's escape, so he jumped right into the icy water.

Fortunately, Tice heard a whippoorwill calling him to safety. Tice looked up and saw a yellow light, the lantern in the window of John Rankin's home.

Tice vanished right before the slave holder's eyes. When the slave holder went home empty-handed, he told everyone an underground railroad came by and picked him up!

Skill Level
Easy

Tools to Gather
6" x 12" ruler
permanent marking pen
wooden iron
point turner
applique foot
invisible thread

	12" Finished Size	6" Finished Size
Background #1		
Sky	(2) 7¼" squares	(2) 4¼" squares
Sky	(2) 5½" squares	(2) 3" squares
Green #1		
Path	(2) 7¼" squares	(2) 4¼" squares
Path	(2) 5½" squares	(2) 3" squares
Fusible Interfacing		
Non-woven	(4) 5½" squares	(4) 3" squares
Lightweight		

Making Drunkard's Path

1. Center and trace four circles on smooth side of lightweight fusible interfacing. Patterns on page 121.

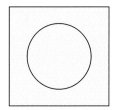

12" Block	4½" circles
6" Block	2½" circles

Place waxed paper in between patterns and fusible to protect pattern from "bleed through."

2. Place bumpy side of interfacing against right side of two smaller Background squares and two smaller Medium/Dark squares. Pin.

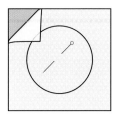
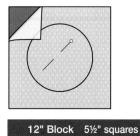

12" Block	5½" squares
6" Block	3" squares

3. Place metal applique foot on sewing machine. If possible, lighten pressure on presser foot.

4. Sew on drawn line with 20 stitches to the inch. Overlap beginning and ending stitches.

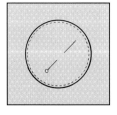

5. Trim circles to ⅛". Cut a slit in middle of interfacing.

6. Turn circle right sides out. Run point turner around inside. Press with wooden iron.

7. Press large squares in fourths. Center Background circles on Medium/Dark squares. Center Medium/Dark circles on Background Squares. Match grainline on circles with grainline on squares.

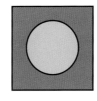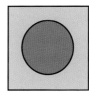

12" Block	7¼" squares
6" Block	4¼" squares

8. Steam press in place. Machine stitch or hand applique.

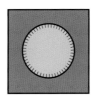

9. Line up squares on gridded cutting mat. Cut squares in half on vertical and horizontal lines.

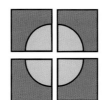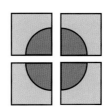

10. Stack all like patches in same direction. There are eight patches in each stack.

11. Flip patch on right over patch on left. Assembly-line sew all eight.

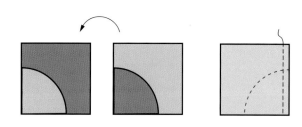

12. Set seams with dark on top, open, and press toward dark.

 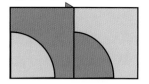

13. Divide patches into two stacks of four. Turn one stack so middle seams lock. Assembly-line sew.

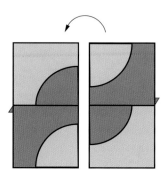

14. At center seam, remove the three straight stitches with a stiletto or seam ripper. Turn over and repeat. See page 21.

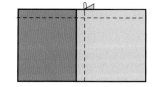 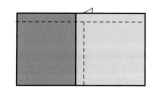

15. Open center seams and push flat to form a tiny four-patch.

16. Press seams clockwise around block.

17. Square up patches.

| 12" Block   6½" squares |
| 6" Block   3½" squares |

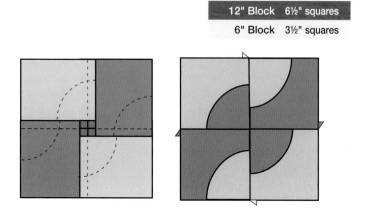

120

18. Lay out patches.

19. Flip right vertical row to left vertical row, and sew.

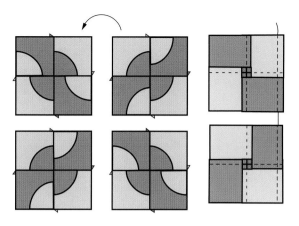

20. Open and sew remaining seam.

21. At center seam, remove the three straight stitches with a stiletto or seam ripper. Turn over and repeat.

22. Open center seams and push flat to form a tiny four-patch.

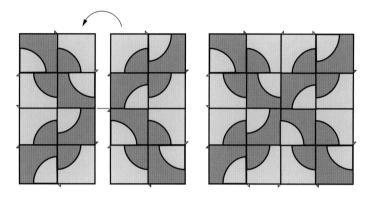

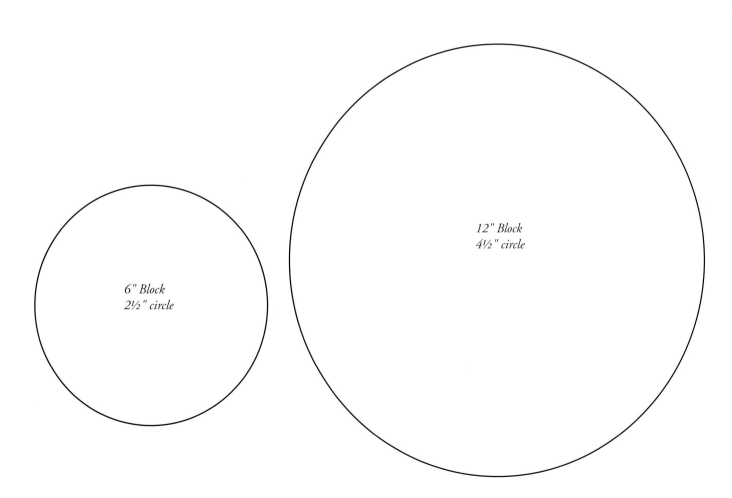

12" Block
4½" circle

6" Block
2½" circle

Sail Boat

The sail boat block is a symbol of safe passage to freedom. It also represents the importance of free black sailors to the Underground Railroad.

Beginning in the 1600s, Africans were imported to New England to work aboard whalers, fishing boats and trading vessels. The knowledge gained by black sailors of northern geography and the languages and customs of free ports made them invaluable members of the Underground Railroad.

Black sailors and ship owners helped many slaves escape directly, hiding them on board their ships and spiriting them away, and indirectly, by passing on directions and sometimes messages from family members awaiting them in freedom. Sailors were often able to exchange information with enslaved blacks at port cities, forming an important link in the grapevine between slaves in the South and their free counterparts in the North. Forbidden to read and write, slaves depended on the knowledge and experiences of those who traveled before them.

When the Compromise of 1850 strengthened the Fugitive Slave Act, allowing slaveholders to retrieve slaves in Northern states and free territories, runaway slaves weren't safe until they reached Canada. Many depended on ships and ferries to cross icy Lake Erie.

Skill Level
Easy

Tools to Gather
6" x 12" ruler
6½" Triangle Square Up ruler
permanent marking pen
stiletto

		12" Finished Size	6" Finished Size
Background #3			
	Sky	(2) 4" squares	(2) 2½" squares
		(3) 3½" squares	(3) 2" squares
		(2) 3½" x 6½"	(2) 2" x 3½"
Red #2			
	Sail	(2) 4" squares	(2) 2½" squares
Brown #2			
	Boat	(1) 3½" x 12½"	(1) 2" x 6½"
Blue #1			
	Water	(1) 3½" x 12½"	(1) 2" x 6½"

123

Making the Sailboat

1. Place two Sky squares right sides together to two Sail squares.

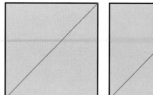

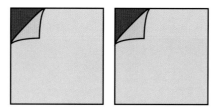

12" Block	4" squares
6" Block	2½" squares

2. Draw diagonal line on wrong side of Sky fabric.

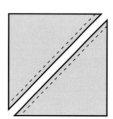

3. Sew ¼" from both sides of diagonal line. Cut on diagonal line.

4. Square three Sail patches with Triangle Square Up ruler. Press seams to dark. *One is extra.*

12" Block	3½" square
6" Block	2" squares

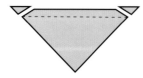

5. Lay out three Sail squares with one Sky square.

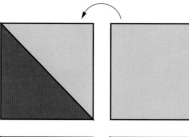

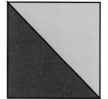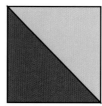

6. Flip patches on right over patches on left. Assembly-line sew.

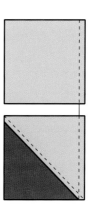

7. Press seams in opposite directions.

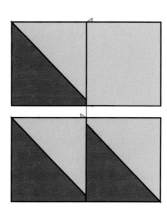

8. Sew two rows together.

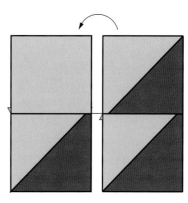

9. Press seams to one side away from Sails.

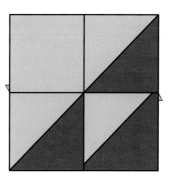

10. Sew Sky piece to each side of Sail.

12" Block	3½" x 6½"
6" Block	2" x 3½"

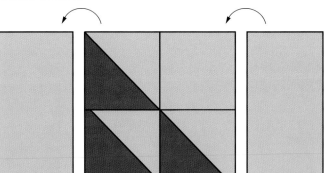

11. Press seams away from Sail.

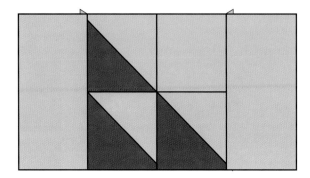

12. Draw diagonal lines on wrong side of two Sky squares.

12" Block	3½" squares
6" Block	2" squares

13. Place one square on each end of Boat.

12" Block	3½" x 12½"
6" Block	2" x 6½"

14. Sew on diagonal lines. Trim excess ¼" from sewn lines.

15. Press seams toward Sky.

16. Lay out Sail, Boat, and Water.

12" Block	3½" x 12½"
6" Block	2" x 6½"

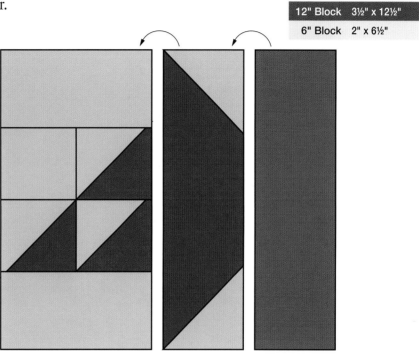

17. Sew together. Press seams away from Sail toward Water.

North Star

The North Star Quilt is the tenth quilt in the secret code passed through the Williams family history. The North Star was the guiding light leading slaves to Canada and freedom. The Big Dipper always points to the North Star, which is in the handle of the Little Dipper.

The North Star was also important to navigation, especially to boat owners who took the slaves from Cleveland or Detroit to Canada.

Perhaps no song is more connected to the Underground Railroad than Follow the Drinking Gourd, secret music they sang behind closed doors.

Another symbolic star is the Star of Bethlehem, which lead the Wisemen to Jesus. This particular Star of Bethlehem has a spot of blood on it, a symbol of bad luck to slaves. They believed throwing a quilt over their roof would bring good luck.

Foller the drinkin' gou'd,
Foller the drinkin' gou'd;
"Foller the drinkin' gou'd."

Foller the Risen Lawd,
Foller the Risen Lawd;
The bes' thing the Wise Man say,
"Foller the Risen Lawd."

When the sun come back,
When the firs' quail call,
Then the time is come,
Foller the drinkin' gou'd.

Chorus:
Foller the drinkin' gou'd,
Foller the drinkin' gou'd;
For the ole man say,
"Foller the drinkin' gou'd."

Skill Level
Easy

Tools to Gather
6" x 12" ruler
6½" Triangle Square Up ruler
Small 3" x 6" Flying Geese Ruler
permanent marking pen
stiletto

		12" Finished Size	6" Finished Size
Background #2			
	Large Star Points	(1) 7½" square	(1) 4½" square
	Large Star Corners	(4) 3½" squares	(4) 2" squares
Background #3			
	Small Star Points	(1) 4½" square	(4) 1¼" x 2"
	Small Star Corners	(4) 2" squares	(4) 1¼" squares
Blue #1			
	Large Star Points	(1) 9" square	(1) 6" square
Red #2			
	Small Star Points	(1) 6" square	(8) 1¼" squares
	Small Star Center	(1) 3½" square	(1) 2" square

Making Eight Star Points for 12" Block

Making Four Large Star Points

1. Place 7½" Background square right sides together and centered on 9" Star Point square.

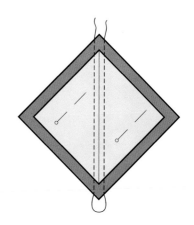

2. Follow instructions for making Star Points on pages 24-27. Trim patches with Small Geese ruler, squaring to 3½" x 6½". Finished size is 3" x 6".

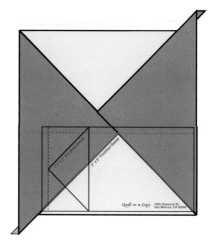

Making Four Small Star Points

1. Place 4½" Background square right sides together and centered on 6" Star Point square.

2. Follow instructions for making Star Points on pages 24-27. Trim patches with Small Geese ruler, squaring to 2" x 3½". Finished size is 1½" x 3".

3. Turn to page 132.

Making Eight Star Points for 6" Block

Making Four Large Star Points

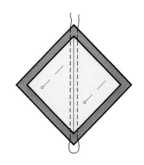

1. Place 4½" Background square right sides together and centered on 6" Star Point square.

2. Follow instructions for making Star Points on pages 24-27. Trim patches with Small Geese ruler, squaring to 2" x 3½". Finished size is 1½" x 3".

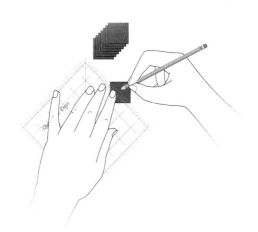

Making Four Small Star Points

1. Turn eight 1¼" squares wrong side up. Draw diagonal line.

   Optional: If available, use Angler in place of drawing diagonal lines.

2. Place one square wrong sides together on 1¼" x 2" Background.

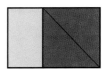

3. Sew on drawn line and trim seam to ¼". Press seam toward Star Points.

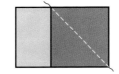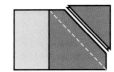

4. Repeat process with remaining Star Points.

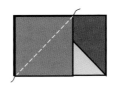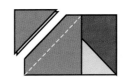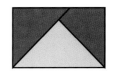

Making Small Star

1. Lay out the Center square, Corner squares and Points.

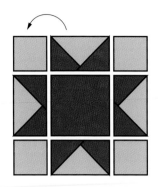

12" Block	Star Points	(4) 2" x 3½"
	Corner Squares	(4) 2" squares
	Center Square	(1) 3½" square
6" Block	Star Points	(4) 1¼" x 2"
	Corner Squares	(4) 1¼" squares
	Center Square	(1) 2" square

2. Flip middle row to left. Assembly-line sew vertical row.

3. Open and add right row.

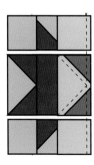

4. Sew first horizontal row, pressing seams toward Star Center, and away from the Star Points.

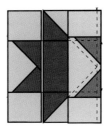

5. Sew second horizontal row, repeating seams. Set seams, open, and press.

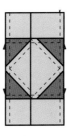

6. Check from wrong side. Horizontal seams should be pressed away from center. Press. Measure your block.

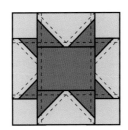

12" Block	6½" square
6" Block	3½" square

Finishing North Star

1. Lay out Small Star with Corners and Star Points. Turn Small Star with last seams in horizontal position.

12" Block	Star	(1) 6½" square
	Corner Squares	(4) 3½" squares
	Star Points	(4) 3½" x 6½"
6" Block	Star	(1) 3½" square
	Corner Squares	(4) 2" squares
	Star Points	(4) 2" x 3½"

2. Flip middle row to left. Check horizontal seams on Star. Assembly-line sew all vertical seams.

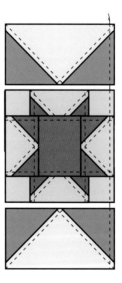

3. Open and add right row.

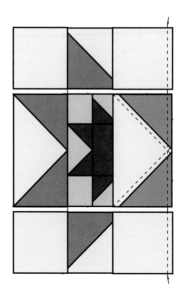

134

4. Sew first horizontal row, pressing seams toward Star, and away from Star Points.

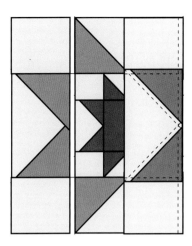

5. Sew second horizontal row, repeating seams. Set seams, open, and press.

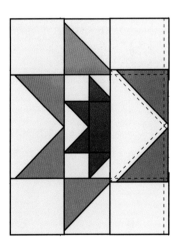

6. Check from wrong side. Horizontal seams should be pressed away from center.

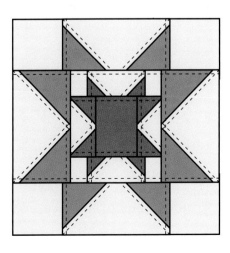

Making Your Story Label

1. Tear out page 159.

2. Load one sheet of Colorfast Printer Fabric™ (June Tailor product number JT900) into paper tray so copying occurs on fabric side of sheet.

3. Place story page into copier and photo copy. If you are making the label for 6" block quilt, reduce size by (.66).

12" Block	8½" square
6" Block	6½" square

4. Remove backing from fabric. Allow ink to dry.

Making a Block for the Front of Your Quilt

1. Square up printed label fabric.

2. **12" Block:** Add a 2½" border on all four sides. Square to 12½".

3. **6" Block:** Square to 6½".

4. Use as sixteenth block in your quilt.

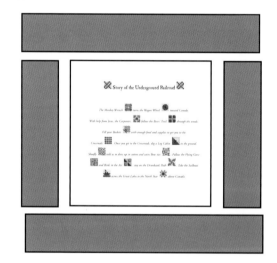

Making a Label for the Back of Your Quilt

1. Sew a hem around all four sides of label.

2. Hand-sew to back of quilt.

Colorfast Printer Fabric™ can be washed by hand or machine in cold water. If machine washing, use gentle cycle. Remove promptly. If soiled, add liquid fabric softener to cold water wash. Lay flat to dry.

Code Quilts

Three small Code Quilts can be used to tell the Underground Railroad story to young and old. Only the ten primary blocks are used.

This yardage chart is for finishing all three Code Quilts. It does not include fabric needed for the blocks. Refer to individual blocks for yardage, cutting, and sewing instructions. Sew blocks together following Plain Lattice instructions, page 142.

Lattice 1 yd

(11) 2½" strips cut into
(32) 2½" x 12½"

Cornerstones ¼ yd

(2) 2½" strips cut into
(25) 2½" squares

Binding 1 yd

(10) 3" strips

Backing 2½ yds

First Code Quilt	34" x 34"
Second Code Quilt	20" x 48"
Third Code Quilt	20" x 48"

Batting 2½ yds of 48" wide batting

First Code Quilt	34" x 34"
Second Code Quilt	20" x 48"
Third Code Quilt	20" x 48"

"The monkey wrench turns
the wagon wheel on the
bear's paw trail to the
crossroads."

Hidden in Plain View, page 82

Monkey Wrench, page 38
Wagon Wheel, page 46
Bear's Paw, page 64
Crossroads, page 78

"Once they got to the crossroads
they dug a log cabin on the ground.
Shoofly told them to dress up in
cotton and satin bow ties . . ."

Hidden in Plain View, page 96

"Flying geese stay on the drunkard's
path and follow the stars."

Hidden in Plain View, page 110

Flying Geese, page 100
Drunkard's Path, page 116
North Star, page 128

Log Cabin, page 84
Shoo-Fly, page 90
Bow Tie, page 96

Squaring Your Blocks

1. Check that each block is a consistent size approximately 12½" or 6½" square.

   For blocks larger than consistent size, sliver trim without trimming away any part of the ¼" seam allowance, or resew a wider seam.

   For blocks smaller than consistent size, check seam widths and pressing.

   If blocks are ¾" smaller than desired size, unsew a few seams and sew again with narrower seam.

2. Do not be concerned if there is a ¼" to ½" variance in block sizes. They can be stretched to size of other blocks.

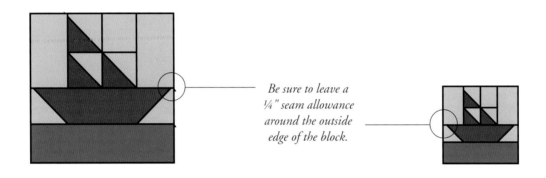

Be sure to leave a ¼" seam allowance around the outside edge of the block.

Use a 12½" Square Up ruler for 12" finished size blocks.

Use a 6½" Triangle Square Up ruler for 6" finished size blocks.

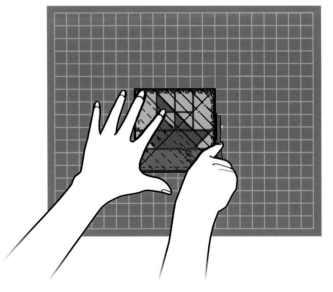

Plain Lattice

12 Block Quilt	12" Blocks	6" Blocks
Lattice	(11) 3½" strips cut into (31) 3½" x size of Block	(6) 2" strips cut into (31) 2" x size of Block
Cornerstones	(2) 3½" strips cut into (20) 3½" squares	(1) 2" strip cut into (20) 2" squares
Border Non-stripe Stripe	(8) 6" strips Four Lengths	(4) 3" strips Four Lengths
Binding	(7) 3" strips	(4) 3" strips

15 Block Quilt		
Lattice	(13) 3½" strips cut into (38) 3½" x size of Block	(7) 2" strips cut into (38) 2" x size of Block
Cornerstones	(2) 3½" strips cut into (24) 3½" squares	(2) 2" strips cut into (24) 2" squares
Border Non-stripe or Stripe	(8) 6" strips Four Lengths	(5) 3" strips Four Lengths
Binding	(8) 3" strips	(5) 3" strips

16 Block Quilt		
Lattice	(14) 3½" strips cut into (40) 3½" x size of Block	(7) 2" strips cut into (40) 2" x size of Block
Cornerstones	(2) 3½" strips cut into (25) 3½" squares	(2) 2" strips cut into (25) 2" squares
Border Non-stripe or Stripe	(8) 6" strips Four Lengths	(5) 3" strips Four Length
Binding	(8) 3" strips	(5) 3" strips

Sewing Blocks Together with Plain Lattice

1. Cut Lattice and Cornerstones following the chart next to your selected layout.

2. Lay out blocks in order with Lattice and Cornerstones.

3. Flip second vertical row right sides together to first vertical row.

4. Stack from bottom up with top Lattice on top of stack.

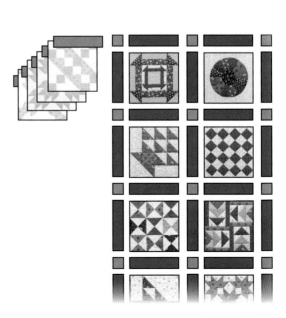

5. Assembly-line sew. Stretch or ease each block to fit the Lattice as you sew. Do not clip connecting threads.

6. Open vertical rows one and two.

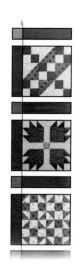

7. Stack third vertical row. Flip pieces in third row right sides together to pieces in second row while assembly-line sewing. Do not clip connecting threads.

8. Repeat with all vertical rows.

9. Lay out quilt. Check that every block, Lattice, and Cornerstone is in its proper position.

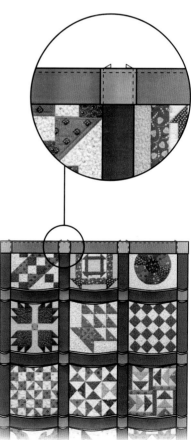

10. Flip top horizontal row right sides together to second horizontal row. Stretch blocks and Lattice to meet, and sew.

11. At Cornerstones, where pieces are joined by threads, match seams carefully. Push seams toward Lattice for locking seams.

12. Continue sewing all horizontal rows.

Flying Geese Lattice

Select a 12, 15, or 16 block setting, and cut pieces according to chart.

12 Block Quilt
for 12" blocks only

Print

    (7) 6" strips cut into

        (40) 6" squares

    (12) 3½" strips cut into

        (14) 3½" x 12½"

        (31) 3½" x 6½"

        (24) 3½" square

Flying Geese

    (3) 4½" strips cut into

        (20) 4½" squares

Flying Geese and Cornerstones

    (3) 4½" strips cut into

        (20) 4½" squares

    (4) 2" strips cut into

        (80) 2" square

Border

Non-stripe

or   (8) 6" strips

Stripe

    Four Lengths

Binding

    (7) 3" strips

15 Block Quilt
for 12" blocks only

Print
    (8) 6" strips cut into
        (48) 6" squares
    (14) 3½" strips cut into
        (16) 3½" x 12½"
        (38) 3½" x 6½"
        (28) 3½" squares

Flying Geese
    (3) 4½" strips cut into
        (24) 4½" squares

Flying Geese and Cornerstones
    (3) 4½" strips cut into
        (24) 4½" squares
    (5) 2" strips cut into
        (96) 2" squares

Border
Non-stripe

or   (8) 6" strips

Stripe

    Four Lengths

Binding
    (8) 3" strips

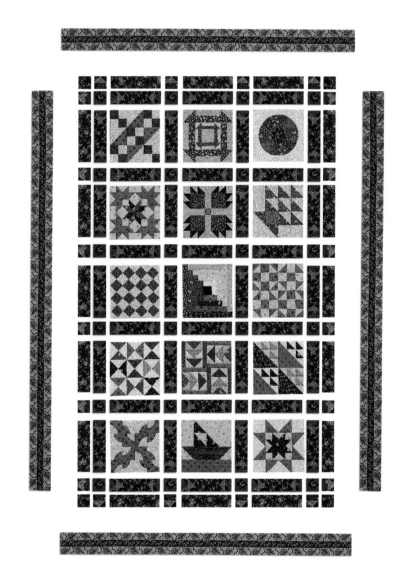

16 Block Quilt
for 12" blocks only

Print

    (9) 6" strips cut into

        (50) 6" squares

    (15) 3½" strips cut into

        (16) 3½" x 12½"

        (40) 3½" x 6½"

        (29) 3½" squares

Flying Geese

    (3) 4½" strips cut into

        (25) 4½" squares

Flying Geese and Cornerstones

    (3) 4½" strips cut into

        (25) 4½" squares

    (5) 2" strips cut into

        (100) 2" squares

Border

Non-stripe

or   (8) 6" strips

Stripe

    Four Lengths

Binding

    (8) 6" strips

Making the Geese

1. Pair two sets of 4½" Flying Geese squares with 6" Print squares. Make Flying Geese following instructions on pages 24 - 27. With the Small Flying Geese ruler, trim geese to 2" x 3½". Finished size is 1½" x 3".

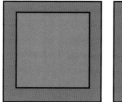

12 Block	40 squares
15 Block	48 squares
16 Block	50 squares

Total Number of Geese from Each Color Combination

12 Block	80 Geese
15 Block	96 Geese
16 Block	100 Geese

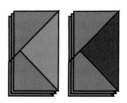

2. Stack all like patches together.

3. Assembly-line sew one Geese patch to second Geese patch.

4. Set and press seams toward left patch.

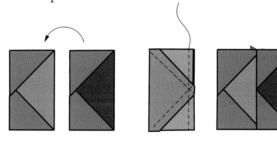

5. Set Flying Geese patches aside for outside rows.

12 Block	18 Geese
15 Block	20 Geese
16 Block	20 Geese

6. Divide the remaining pairs into two equal stacks for Lattice.

12 Block	62 pairs into two stacks of 31
15 Block	76 pairs into two stacks of 38
16 Block	82 pairs into two stacks of 41

Making the Lattice Strips

1. Layer 3½" x 6½" Print fabric right sides up.

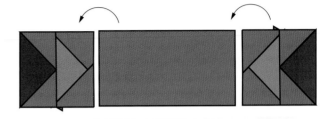

Twelve Block	31 strips
Fifteen Block	38 strips
16 Block	41 strips

2. Place a stack of Geese pairs on each end of Print fabric. Turn points in.

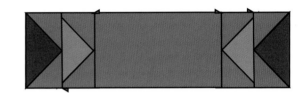

3. Assembly-line sew Geese to Lattice. Set and press seams toward Lattice.

Making the Cornerstones

1. Draw a diagonal line on wrong side of 2" squares.

   Optional: If available, use the Angler in place of drawing diagonal lines.

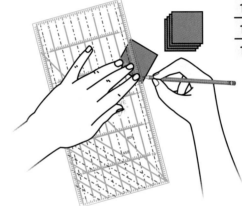

12 Block	80 squares
15 Block	96 squares
16 Block	100 squares

2. Place a 2" square on two opposite corners of 3½" Print fabrics, wrong sides together. Sew on the drawn line.

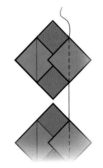

12 Block	20 squares
15 Block	24 squares
16 Block	25 squares

3. Trim to ¼". Press seams toward Geese fabric.

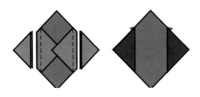

4. Sew 2" squares to remaining 3½" corners.

5. Trim to ¼". Press seams toward Geese patches.

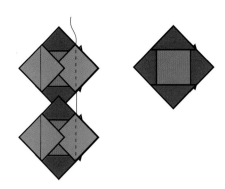

Completing the Quilt

1. Lay out the 3½" Cornerstones, Geese patches, Lattice, and blocks.

2. Assembly-line sew vertical rows together.

3. Set seams and press toward Lattice.

4. Sew remaining rows together.

5. Press seams away from block rows.

Finishing Your Quilt

Adding Borders

1. Cut Border strips according to Yardage Charts.

2. Trim away selvages at a right angle.

3. Lay first strip right side up. Lay second strip right sides to it. Backstitch, stitch, and backstitch again.

4. Continue assembly-line sewing all short ends together into long pieces.

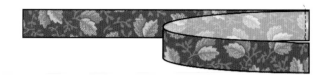

5. Cut Border pieces the average length of both sides.

6. Pin and sew to sides. Fold out and press seams toward Border.

7. Measure the width and cut Border pieces for top and bottom. Pin and sew.

8. Press seams toward Border.

Layering the Quilt

1. Spread out Backing on a large table or floor area, right side down. Clamp fabric to edge of table with quilt clips, or tape Backing to the floor. Do not stretch Backing.

2. Layer the Batting on the Backing and pat flat.

3. With quilt right side up, center on the Backing. Smooth until all layers are flat. Clamp or tape outside edges.

Safety Pinning

1. Place pin covers on 1" safety pins. Safety pin through all layers three to five inches apart. Pin away from where you plan to quilt.

2. Catch tip of pin in grooves on pinning tool, and close pins.

3. Use pinning tool to open pins when removing them. Store pins opened.

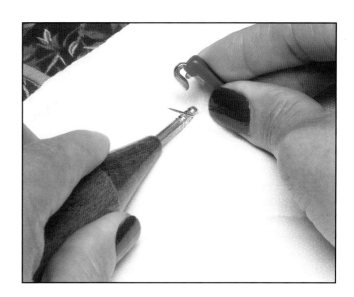

"Stitch in the Ditch" along Lattice and Borders

1. Thread your machine with matching thread or invisible thread. If you use invisible thread, loosen your top tension. Match the bobbin thread to the Backing.

2. Attach your walking foot, and lengthen the stitch to 8 to 10 stitches per inch or 3.5 on computerized machines.

3. Tightly roll quilt from one long side to center vertical Lattice. Place hands on quilt in triangular shape, and spread seams open. Stitch in the ditch along seam lines and anchor blocks and border.

4. Roll quilt in opposite direction, and stitch in ditch along seam lines.

Quilting Blocks with Darning Foot

1. Attach darning foot to sewing machine. Drop feed dogs or cover feed dogs with a plate. No stitch length is required as you control the length. Use a fine needle and invisible or regular thread in the top and regular thread to match the Backing in the bobbin. Loosen top tension if using invisible thread. Use needle down position.

2. Plan how to stitch, covering as many seams continuously as possible.

3. Place hands flat on block. Bring bobbin thread up on seam line.

4. Lock stitch and clip thread tails. Free motion stitch in the ditch around block. Keep top of block at top. Sew sideways, back and forth, without turning quilt.

5. Lock stitch and cut threads. Continue with remaining blocks.

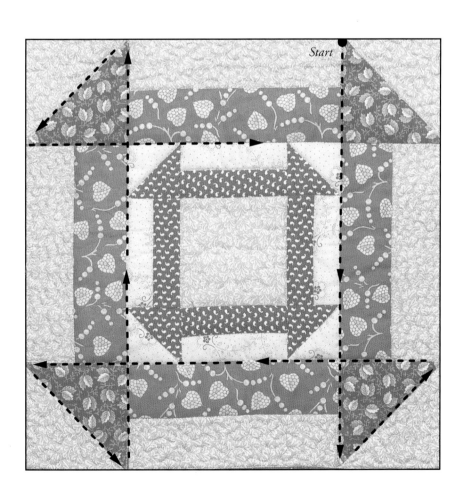

Binding

Use a walking foot attachment and regular thread on top
and in the bobbin to match the Binding.

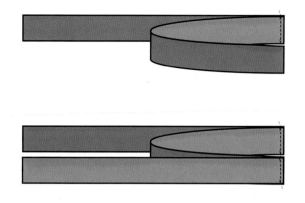

1. Square off the selvage edges, and sew
   3" Binding strips together lengthwise.

2. Fold and press in half with wrong
   sides together.

3. Line up the raw edges of the folded Binding with
   the raw edges of the quilt in the middle of one side.

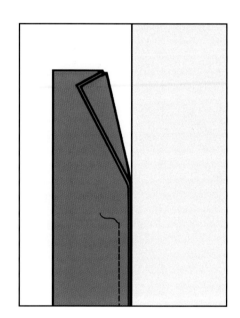

4. Begin stitching 4" from the end of the Binding. Sew
   with 10 stitches per inch, or 3.0 to 3.5. Sew ⅜"
   from edge, or width of walking foot.

5. At the corner, stop the stitching ⅜" in from the edge
   with the needle in the fabric. Raise the presser foot and
   turn the quilt to the next side. Put the foot back down.

6. Stitch backwards at an angle off the edge of the Binding.

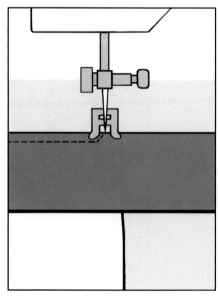

7. Raise the foot, and pull the quilt forward slightly.

8. Fold the Binding strip straight up on the diagonal. Fingerpress the diagonal fold.

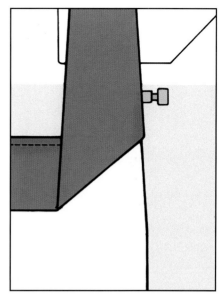

9. Fold the Binding strip straight down with the diagonal fold underneath. Line up the top of the fold with the raw edge of the Binding underneath.

10. Begin sewing from the edge.

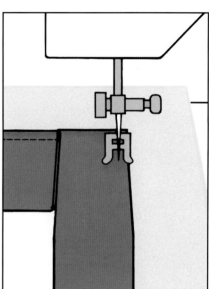

11. Continue stitching and mitering the corners around the outside of the quilt.

12. Stop stitching 4" from where the ends will overlap.

13. Line up the two ends of Binding. Trim the excess with a ½" overlap.

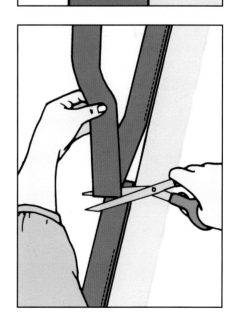

14. Open out the folded ends and pin right sides together. Sew a ¼" seam.

15. Continue to stitch the Binding in place.

16. Trim the Batting and Backing up to the raw edges of the Binding.

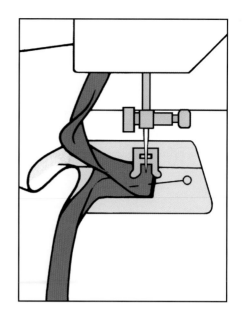

17. Fold the Binding to the back side of the quilt. Pin in place so that the folded edge on the Binding overlaps the stitching line. Tuck in the excess fabric at each miter on the diagonal.

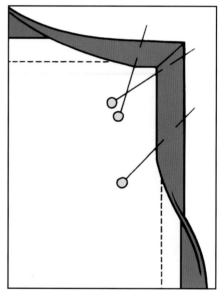

18. From the right side, "stitch in the ditch" using invisible thread on the front side, and bobbin thread to match the Binding on the back side. Catch the folded edge of the Binding on the back side with the stitching. Optional: Hand stitch Binding in place.

19. Sew identification label on the Back. Identification label is on page 159.

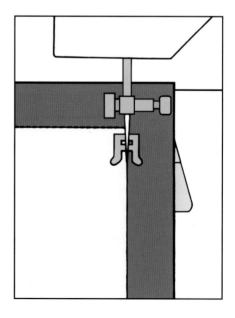

Index

Acknowledgements

A gracious thank you to these dedicated women

Cindee Ferris
Lori Forsythe
Patricia Knoechel
Amie Potter
Bette Rhodabach
Aiko Rogers
Carol Selepec
Sonya Price
Teresa Varnes

Resources

Blackson, Charles L.
The Underground Railroad; Dramatic First Hand Accounts of Daring Escapes to Freedom.
Berkley Books, New York, NY. 1987

Bradford, Sarah.
Harriet Tubman, The Moses of Her People.
Applewood Books. Bedford, MA. 1886.

Ferrero, Pat, and Elaine Hedges, and Julie Silber.
Hearts and Hands, The Influence of Women & Quilts on American Society.
The Quilt Digest Press, San Francisco, CA. 1987.

Fry, Gladys-Marie.
Stitched from the Soul, Slave Quilts from the Ante-bellum South.
Dutton Studio Books, New York. Museum of American Folk Art, New York, NY. 1990.

Guccione, Leslie Davis.
Come Morning.
Carolrhoda Books, Inc. Minneapolis, MN. 1995.

Hansen, Ellen.
The Underground Railroad: Life on the Road to Freedom.
Discovery Enterprises, Ltd., Carlisle, MA. 1995.

Hurmence, Belinda.
Slavery Time When I Was Chillun.
G. P. Putnam's Sons. New York, NY. 1997.

Tobin, Jacqueline L. and Raymond G. Dobard, Ph. D.
Hidden In Plain View; A Secret Story of Quilts and the Underground Railroad.
Anchor Books, New York, NY. 1999.

Order Information

Quilt in a Day books offer a wide range of techniques and are directed toward a variety of skill levels. If you do not have a quilt shop in your area, you may write or call for a complete catalog and current price list of all books and patterns published by Quilt in a Day®, Inc.

Quilt in a Day 1955 Diamond St. San Marcos, CA 92078
800 777-4852 • order online www.quiltinaday.com

Story of the Underground Railroad

The Monkey Wrench turns the Wagon Wheel toward Canada.

With help from Jesus, the Carpenter, follow the Bears' Trail through the woods.

Fill your Baskets with enough food and supplies to get you to the

Crossroads . Once you get to the Crossroads, dig a Log Cabin in the ground.

Shoofly told us to dress up in cotton and satin Bow Ties . Follow the Flying Geese

 and Birds in the Air , stay on the Drunkard's Path . Take the Sailboat

 across the Great Lakes to the North Star above Canada.

12" Basket
Background #1
(1) 8" square
Handle

12" Railroad
Background #1
(1) 2½" x 30"
Four-Patches

12" Log Cabin
Background #2
(1) 1¾" x 3¾"
1st Light

12" Basket
Background #1
(1) 7" square
Bottom

12" Log Cabin
Background #1
(1) 1¾" x 5"
2nd Light

12" Flying Geese
Background #3
(1) 7" square
Sky

12" Flying Geese
Background #1
(1) 7" square
Sky

12" Log Cabin
Background #1
(1) 1¾" x 6 1/4"
2nd Light

12" Birds
Background #3
(1) 6" square
Sky

12" Drunkard's Path
Background #1
(2) 7¼" squares
Sky

12" Wagon Wheel
Background #2
(1) 13" square
Background

12" Shoo-Fly
Background #3
(2) 6" squares
Triangles

12" Drunkard's Path
Background #1
(2) 5½" squares
Sky

12" North Star
Background #2
(1) 7½" square
Sky

12" Carpenter's Wheel
Background #3
(2) 4½" squares
Flying Geese

12" Crossroads
Background #1
(3) 5½" squares
Side Triangles

12" Birds
Background #2
(1) 6" square
Sky

12" North Star
Background #3
(1) 4½" square
Small Star Sky

12" Railroad
Background #1
(1) 5" x 10"
Triangle Pieced Sqs

12" Bow Tie
Background #2
(5) 5½" squares
Background

12" Sailboat
Background #3
(2) 4" squares
Sky

12" Basket
Background #1
(2) 3½" x 6½"
Sides

12" North Star
Background #2
(4) 3½" squares
Large Star Corners

12" Sailboat
Background #3
(3) 3½" squares
Sky

12" Crossroads
Background #1
(2) 3½" squares
Corners

12" Birds
Background #2
(3) 2½" x 3 1/4"
Sky

12" Sailboat
Background #3
(2) 3½" x 6½"
Sky

12" Crossroads
Background #1
(9) 2½" squares
Crossroads

12" Log Cabin
Background #2
(1) 1¾" x 2½"
1st Light

12" Carpenter's Wheel
Background #3
(4) 3½" squares
Star Points/Flying Geese

12" Blocks

12" Shoo-Fly
Background #3
(10) 2½" squares
Squares

12" Bear's Paw
Background #4
(2) 6" squares
Claws

12" Monkey Wrench
Red #1
(1) 2½" x 5"
Corners

12" Birds
Background #3
(3) 2½" x 3¼"
Sky

12" Monkey Wrench
Background #4
(1) 4" x 8"
Corners

12" Log Cabin
Red #1
(1) 1¾" x 7½"
4th Dark

12" Monkey Wrench
Background #3
(1) 2½" x 5"
Corners

12" Monkey Wrench
Background #4
(1) 3½" square
Center Square

12" Flying Geese
Red #1
(4) 1½" x 7"
Sides

12" North Star
Background #3
(4) 2" squares
Small Star Corners

12" Bear's Paw
Background #4
(4) 2¼" squares
Corners

12" Monkey Wrench
Red #1
(1) 1¼" x 15"
Sides

12" Carpenter's Wheel
Background #3
(8) 2" squares
Wheel Rim and Corners

12" Bear's Paw
Background #4
(4) 2" x 5¾"
Dividing Strips

12" North Star
Red #2
(1) 6" square
Small Star Points

12" Carpenter's Wheel
Background #3
(4) 2" x 3½"
Sides

12" Log Cabin
Background #4
(1) 2" x 10"
4th Light

12" Birds
Red #2
(1) 6" square
Birds

12" Log Cabin
Background #3
(1) 1¾" x 7½"
3rd Light

12" Log Cabin
Background #4
(1) 2" x 11¼"
4th Light

12" Bow Tie
Red #2
(1) 5½" square
Bow Ties

12" Log Cabin
Background #3
(1) 1¾" x 8¾"
3rd Light

12" Monkey Wrench
Background #4
(2) 2" x 14"
Sides

12" Sailboat
Red #2
(2) 4" squares
Sail

12" Monkey Wrench
Background #3
(1) 1¼" x 15"
Sides

12" Crossroads
Red #1
(16) 2½" squares
Crossroads

12" North Star
Red #2
(1) 3½" square
Small Star Center

12" Flying Geese
Background #4
(1) 7" square
Sky

12" Wagon Wheel
Red #1
(1) 5" x 6"
Spokes

12" Carpenter's Wheel
Red #2
(1) 2½" x 5"
Star Center

12" Blocks

12" Carpenter's Wheel
Red #2
(4) 2" squares
Star Points

12" Log Cabin
Red #2
(1) 1¾" x 6¼"
3rd Dark

12" Wagon Wheel
Red #3
(1) 5" x 6"
Spokes

12" Bear's Paw
Red #3
(4) 4" squares
Paws

12" Log Cabin
Red #3
(1) 1¾" x 5"
2nd Dark

12" Wagon Wheel
Brown #1
(1) 5" x 6"
Spokes

12" Monkey Wrench
Brown #1
(1) 4" x 8"
Corners

12" Log Cabin
Brown #1
(1) 2" x 13"
8th Dark

12" Birds
Brown #2
(1) 7" x 8"
Nests

12" Wagon Wheel
Brown #2
(1) 5" square
Center

12" Log Cabin
Brown #2
(1) 2" x 11¼"
7th Dark

12" Sailboat
Brown #2
(1) 3½" x 12½"
Boat

12" Railroad
Brown #3
(1) 2½" x 30"
Four-Patches

12" Bow Tie
Brown #3
(1) 5½" square
Ties

12" Flying Geese
Brown #3
(1) 5½" square
Geese

12" North Star
Blue #1
(1) 9" square
Large Star Points

12" Birds
Blue #1
(1) 7" x 8"
Nests

12" Carpenter's Wheel
Blue #1
(2) 6" squares
Flying Geese

12" Carpenter's Wheel
Blue #1
(8) 2" squares
Flying Geese

12" Carpenter's Wheel
Blue #1
(4) 2" squares
Wheel Rim

12" Carpenter's Wheel
Blue #1
(4) 2" x 3½"
Wheel Rim Rectangle

12" Bear's Paw
Blue #1
(1) 2" square
Center

12" Basket
Blue #1
(1) 3½" square
Base

12" Sailboat
Blue #1
(1) 3½" x 12½"
Water

12" Log Cabin
Blue #1
(1) 1¾" x 3¾"
1st Dark

12" Flying Geese
Blue #1
(4) 1½" x 7"
Geese

12" Basket
Blue #2
(1) 8" square
Handle

12" Bow Tie
Blue #2
(1) 5½" square
Bow Ties

12" Flying Geese
Blue #2
(1) 5½ " square
Geese

12" Wagon Wheel
Blue #2
(1) 5" x 6"
Spokes

12" Blocks

12" Basket
Blue #2
(1) 4" square
Feet

12" Railroad
Green #1
(1) 5" x 10"
Triangle Pieced Squares

12" Log Cabin
Blue #2
(1) 1¾" x 10"
6th Dark

12" Wagon Wheel
Green #1
(1) 5" x 6"
Spokes

12" Wagon Wheel
Blue #3
(1) 5" x 6"
Spokes

12" Shoo-Fly
Green #1
(10) 2½" squares
Squares

12" Monkey Wrench
Blue #3
(2) 2" x 14"
Sides

12" Log Cabin
Green #1
(1) 1¾" x 8¾"
5th Dark

12" Carpenter's Wheel
Blue #3
(1) 2½" x 5"
Star Center

12" Birds
Green #2
(1) 6" square
Birds

12" Carpenter's Wheel
Blue #3
(4) 2" squares
Star Points

12" Bow Tie
Green #2
(1) 5½" square
Ties

12" Drunkard's Path
Green #1
(2) 7¼" squares
Path

12" Flying Geese
Green #2
(1) 5½" square
Geese

12" Shoo-Fly
Green #1
(2) 6" squares
Triangles

12" Bear's Paw
Green #3
(2) 6" squares
Claws

12" Bow Tie
Green #1
(1) 5½" square
Bow Ties

12" Log Cabin
Black
(1) 2½" square
Center

12" Drunkard' Path
Green #1
(2) 5½" squares
Path

6" Blocks

6" Basket
Background #1
(1) 5" square
Handle

6" Crossroads
Background #1
(9) 1½" squares
Crossroads

6" Log Cabin
Background #2
(1) 1 1/8" x 2 1/8"
1st Light

6" Basket
Background #1
(1) 4" square
Bottom

6" Railroad
Background #1
(1) 1½" x 20"
Four-Patches

6" Birds
Background #3
(1) 4" square
Sky

6" Drunkard's Path
Background #1
(2) 4¼" squares
Sky

6" Flying Geese
Background #1
(8) 1½ " squares
Sky

6" Shoo-Fly
Background #3
(2) 4" squares
Triangles

6" Drunkard's Path
Background #1
(2) 3" squares
Sky

6" Wagon Wheel
Background #2
(1) 7" square
Background

6" Sailboat
Background #3
(2) 2½" squares
Sky

6" Railroad
Background #1
(1) 3" x 6"
Triangle Pieced Sqs.

6" North Star
Background #2
(1) 4½" square
Sky

6" Sailboat
Background #3
(2) 2½" x 3½"
Sky

6" Crossroads
Background #1
(3) 3½" squares
Side Triangles

6" Birds
Background #2
(1) 4" square
Sky

6" Sailboat
Background #3
(3) 2" squares
Sky

6" Basket
Background #1
(2) 2" x 3½"
Sides

6" Bow Tie
Background #2
(5) 3½" squares
Background

6" Carpenter's Wheel
Background #3
(4) 2" squares
Flying Geese

6" Log Cabin
Background #1
(1) 1⅛" x 2¾"
2nd Light

6" North Star
Background #2
(4) 2" squares
Large Star Corners

6" Monkey Wrench
Background #3
(1) 2" x 4"
Corners

6" Log Cabin
Background #1
(1) 1⅛" x 3⅜"
2nd Light

6" Birds
Background #2
(3) 1½" x 2¼"
Sky

6" Flying Geese
Background #3
(8) 1½" squares
Sky

6" Crossroads
Background #1
(2) 2" squares
Corners

6" Log Cabin
Background #2
(1) 1⅛" x 1½"
1st Light

6" Shoo-Fly
Background #3
(10) 1½" squares
Squares

6" Blocks

6" Birds
Background #3
(3) 1½" x 2¼"
Sky

6" North Star
Background #3
(4) 1½" x 2"
Sky

6" North Star
Background #3
(4) 1¼" squares
Small Star Corners

6" Carpenter's Wheel
Background #3
(8) 1¼" squares
Wheel Rim and Corners

6" Carpenter's Wheel
Background #3
(8) 1¼" x 2"
Flying Geese

6" Carpenter's Wheel
Background #3
(4) 1¼" x 2"
Sides

6" Log Cabin
Background #3
(1) 1⅛" x 4"
3rd Light

6" Log Cabin
Background #3
(1) 1⅛" x 4⅝"
3rd Light

6" Monkey Wrench
Background #3
(1) ⅞" x 9"
Sides

6" Bear's Paw
Background #4
(2) 4" squares
Claws

6" Monkey Wrench
Background #4
(1) 2½" x 5"
Corners

6" Monkey Wrench
Background #4
(1) 2" square
Center Square

6" Flying Geese
Background #4
(8) 1½" squares
Sky

6" Bear's Paw
Background #4
(4) 1⅜" squares
Corners

6" Log Cabin
Background #4
(1) 1⅜" x 5¼"
4th Light

6" Log Cabin
Background #4
(1) 1⅜" x 6⅛"
4th Light

6" Bear's Paw
Background #4
(4) 1¼" x 3⅛"
Dividing Strips

6" Monkey Wrench
Background #4
(1) 1¼" x 15"
Sides

6" Wagon Wheel
Red #1
(1) 3" x 4"
Spokes

6" Crossroads
Red #1
(16) 1½" squares
Crossroads

6" Monkey Wrench
Red #1
(1) 2" x 4"
Corners

6" Log Cabin
Red #1
(1) 1⅛" x 4"
4th Dark

6" Flying Geese
Red #1
(4) 1" x 4"
Sides

6" Monkey Wrench
Red #1
(1) ⅞" x 9"
Sides

6" Birds
Red #2
(1) 4" square
Birds

6" Bow Tie
Red #2
(1) 3½" square
Bow Ties

6" Sailboat
Red #2
(2) 2½" squares
Sail

6" North Star
Red #2
(1) 2" square
Small Star Center

6" Carpenter's Wheel
Red #2
(1) 2" x 4"
Star Center

6" Carpenter's Wheel
Red #2
(4) 1¼" squares
Star Points

6" Blocks

6" North Star
Red #2
(8) 1¼" square
Small Star Points

6" Sailboat
Brown #2
(1) 2" x 6½"
Boat

6" Carpenter's Wheel
Blue #1
(8) 1¼" squares
Flying Geese

6" Log Cabin
Red #2
(1) 1⅛" x 3⅜"
3rd Dark

6" Log Cabin
Brown #2
(1) 1⅜" x 6⅛"
7th Dark

6" Carpenter's Wheel
Blue #1
(4) 1¼" squares
Wheel Rim

6" Wagon Wheel
Red #3
(1) 3" x 4"
Spokes

6" Bow Tie
Brown #3
(1) 3½" square
Ties

6" Carpenter's Wheel
Blue #1
(4) 1¼" x 2"
Wheel Rim Rectangle

6" Bear's Paw
Red #3
(4) 2¼" squares
Paws

6" Railroad
Brown #3
(1) 1½" x 20"
Four-Patches

6" Bear's Paw
Blue #1
(1) 1¼" square
Center

6" Log Cabin
Red #3
(1) 1⅛" x 2¾"
2nd Dark

6" Flying Geese
Brown #3
(4) 1½" x 2½"
Geese

6" Log Cabin
Blue #1
(1) 1 1/8" x 2 1/8"
1st Dark

6" Wagon Wheel
Brown #1
(1) 3" x 4"
Spokes

6" North Star
Blue #1
(1) 6" square
Large Star Points

6" Flying Geese
Blue #1
(4) 1" x 4"
Geese

6" Monkey Wrench
Brown #1
(1) 2½" x 5"
Corners

6" Birds
Blue #1
(1) 4" x 5"
Nests

6" Basket
Blue #2
(1) 5" square
Handle

6" Log Cabin
Brown #1
(1) 1⅜" x 7"
8th Dark

6" Basket
Blue #1
(1) 2" square
Base

6" Wagon Wheel
Blue #2
(1) 3" x 4"
Spokes

6" Birds
Brown #2
(1) 4" x 5"
Nests

6" Sailboat
Blue #1 (1) 2" x 6½"
Water

6" Bow Tie
Blue #2
(1) 3½" square
Ties

6" Wagon Wheel
Brown #2
(1) 2½" square
Center

6" Carpenter's Wheel
Blue #1
(16) 1¼" squares
Flying Geese

6" Flying Geese
Blue #2
(4) 1½" x 2½"
Geese

6" Blocks

6" Basket
Blue #2
(1) 2½" square
Feet

6" Drunkard's Path
Green #1
(2) 3" squares
Path

6" Log Cabin
Blue #2
(1) 1⅛" x 5¼"
6th Dark

6" Railroad
Green #1
(1) 3" x 6"
Triangle Pieced Squares

6" Wagon Wheel
Blue #3
(1) 3" x 4"
Spokes

6" Log Cabin
Green #1
(1) 1⅛" x 4⅝"
5th Dark

6" Carpenter's Wheel
Blue #3
(1) 2" x 4"
Star Center

6" Shoo-Fly
Green #1
(10) 1½" squares
Squares

6" Monkey Wrench
Blue #3
(1) 1¼" x 15"
Sides

6" Birds
Green #2
(1) 4" square
Birds

6" Carpenter's Wheel
Blue #3
(4) 1¼" squares
Star Points

6" Bow Tie
Green #2
(1) 3½" square
Ties

6" Drunkard's Path
Green #1
(2) 4¼" squares
Path

6" Flying Geese
Green #2
(4) 1½" x 2½"
Geese

6" Shoo-Fly
Green #1
(2) 4" squares
Triangles

6" Bear's Paw
Green #3
(2) 4" squares
Claws

6" Wagon Wheel
Green #1
(1) 3" x 4"
Spokes

6" Log Cabin
Black
(1) 1½" square
Center

6" Bow Tie
Green #1
(1) 3½" square
Bow Tie

81" x 81"

Bette Rhodabach

New quilter Bette Rhodabach is proud of her sixteen block Underground Railroad quilt, especially when sharing accompanying stories with her family. Sue Bouchard helped Bette select the bright rose border; cheery reds, bright blues, and sage greens quickly followed. Bette found the bright colors more pleasing in comparison with the dull colors of that time period. Recently a newcomer to California, Bette enjoyed Sue's class, making friends and learning new techniques with each block. She said, "Those 200 geese for the Flying Geese Lattice could have been daunting, but if you just follow the directions, they will turn out perfect!"

The North Star guided Bette to safety in a new home, and new hobby. You too will enjoy the same journey!